THE
NEXT
LEVEL

THE
NEXT
LEVEL

Essential Strategies for Achieving Breakthrough Growth

JAMES B. WOOD
with Larry Rothstein

PERSEUS BOOKS
Cambridge, Massachusetts

LOC Catalog Card Number available through the Library of Congress

ISBN 0-7382-0159-6

Perseus Books is a member of the Perseus Books Group.

Jacket design by Andrew Newman
Text design by Karen Savary
Set in 11.5-point Adobe Garamond by Vicki L. Hochstedler

1 2 3 4 5 6 7 8 9 10——03 02 01 00 99

Perseus Books are available at special discounts for bulk purchases in the U.S. by corporations, institutions, and other organizations. For more information, please contact the Special Markets Department at HarperCollins Publishers, 10 East 53rd Street, New York, NY 10022, or call 1-212-207-7528.

Find Perseus Books on the World Wide Web at
http://www.perseusbooks.com

To Ruth—for always believing in me.
You are my life's inspiration.

CONTENTS

PREFACE

EVERYONE WANTS THEIR BUSINESS TO GROW. I HAVE spoken with thousands of CEOs, managers and business leaders over the past 10 years, and have yet to meet one who tells me, "We just want our company to stay the same as it's always been." Some entrepreneurs have grandiose visions of building an empire; others simply want steady progress in sales and profits. But they all want growth. The question is, if growth is such a universal quest among businesses and organizations across the world, why are some companies growing and some just struggling to get by? Is it dynamic leadership? The right product or technology? Or is it just plain luck? *Who or what is responsible for an organization's growth or failure to grow?*

I have had the privilege of working in a great laboratory of sorts, at *Inc.* magazine. Between 1991 and 1998, I have consulted with hundreds of CEOs who confided to me their most intimate business concerns. I have listened to their common fears and dreams, their frustrations and challenges. This experience has provided me with many insights about the pitfalls and problems of business growth.

As I grappled with finding a "solution" to the question of what causes growth, I consulted the wisdom of academic research on this topic. Although I uncovered some interesting and relevant information, I found little that was of practical use. Most advice was geared toward specific aspects of business functions or disciplines: customer service, leadership, quality improvement, marketing, etc. Each idea might incrementally improve a company, but *would not, if pursued on its own foster long-term growth.*

At a recent conference, a speaker described more than 50 management fads that have swept the business world in the last 15 years. The fact is that taken on their own and in large doses, these management elixirs will not assure a company's growth, nor will they account for the complexities that are confronted by business leaders every day as they face the difficulties and challenges of managing their companies. Long-term business success does not come down to just one thing. Business growth is more a result of doing *many things* right. And that's why it is so challenging.

The successful growth companies, I found, were less caught up in the latest management fad than committed to doing a good job at managing the basic fundamentals of business. And it is these basics of business management that often get overlooked or lost in the shuffle as a company deals with the increasingly complicated landscape of competing in the twenty-first century.

THE PURPOSE OF THIS BOOK

The goal of *The Next Level* is to provide you with a systematic framework for making the right decisions to achieve breakthrough growth. It is based on the practical realities of business, taken from the laboratory of *Inc.*: the companies written about in the magazine and those that make up the *Inc.* 500 lists, the company leaders who read the magazine, those who attend *Inc.*'s conferences, and those who work with the magazine's Growth Strategy Consulting Group.

In the process of developing the material presented in this book, I tested a number of theories and models against real businesses, real people, and real problems. The end result is a set of tools and concepts, presented in this book, that not only provides a model for viewing business growth but will also allow you to personally assess *your own* company's health.

In the pages that follow, I describe a powerful process that helps business owners, managers, directors, and executives analyze their organization's growth potential, identify constraints to future growth, and put into practice the critical behaviors and actions that ensure long-term success.

The Next Level starts by reviewing the common stages of corporate growth. It then provides you with a diagnostic tool, a written survey called the Growth Strategy Analysis, which allows you to assess your organization's strengths and weaknesses within the context of *future* growth. Next, the five critical Growth Drivers are discussed: Market Intelligence, Strategic Leadership, Clarity of Purpose, Strategic Planning, and Internal Infrastructure. Each Growth Driver is discussed in depth, and practical advice is given on how to achieve competency in each area.

The book is built around these insights and the Growth Strategy Analysis. The chapters are the following:

Chapter 1. The Growth Curve

This chapter explains that growth cannot be approached as a continuous straight line; rather it is more accurately described as an S-curve. A company cannot move from one level of growth to the next by following the same path. There is a fundamental break between the first growth curve and the next. To begin the second growth curve, a company must begin to generate new actions, strategies, and behaviors.

Chapter 2. Breaking Through—Managing the Transition to the Next Level

Companies that are in the transition from one level of growth to the next usually experience chaos, confusion, and tension. Several corporate behaviors are characteristic at this stage. They include the Treadmill Mentality, Management by Insanity, Rearview-Mirror Management, Management by ESP, and Midas Touch Management.

Having identified these corporate behaviors within your own organization, you can conduct the Growth Strategy Analysis. The analysis, consisting of eight questions in five categories, enables you to assess how well your company is doing in terms of the five Growth Drivers. For each category, you total the results and determine whether your company is either ahead of the curve, getting by, or behind the pack. On the basis of these results, you can determine your company's strengths and weaknesses and decide which of the following five chapters should be studied first.

Chapter 3. Market Intelligence

This chapter focuses on a company's ability to perceive and adapt to changes in the external marketplace, the first Growth Driver. It compares and contrasts the Market Intelligence of stalled versus growing companies and provides specific steps for building market intelligence in your own company through such techniques as strategic listening and customer advisory boards.

Chapter 4. Strategic Leadership

The second Growth Driver is the CEO's approach to leading the business, which must alter as a company grows. He or she must shift from an attitude of "running the business" to one of "building the organization"—being a strategic leader. This chapter analyzes the symptoms of a CEO who is not making the transition to strategic leader, and then outlines the critical responsibilities of a CEO in a growing company, such as setting the corporate strategies and communicating effectively with the entire organization.

Chapter 5. Clarity of Purpose

One of the critical success factors is your employees—but without a shared understanding of the company's unique identity and significance in the world, along with a detailed picture of the future, they cannot contribute to its growth and success. Hence the importance of the third Growth Driver, clarity of purpose.

The exercises and case examples in this chapter will help you clarify and focus yourself and others in the company. For example, imagine yourself on the cover of *Inc.* magazine five years in the future, featured as the "*Inc.* 500 CEO of the Year." What would the article say? How did your company grow? What is it like to work for the company? What is your company's story?

Chapter 6. Strategic Planning

This chapter, on the fourth Growth Driver, focuses on a company's ability to develop a high-impact, collaborative plan for achieving future goals. Planning is a key discipline that will help a company make the transition from mom-and-pop shop to a professionally managed firm. This plan should consist of specific tactics, actions, and measures of accountability, and should be communicated throughout the organization.

This chapter gives a set of questions to initiate planning and a format for the planning process followed by ten reasons why planning works.

Chapter 7. Internal Infrastructure

The final Growth Driver refers to the development of organizational and operational structures and systems to support a company's business strategies. If an adequate infrastructure is not in place, it is extremely difficult to achieve any of a company's growth goals.

This chapter identifies the most common stumbling blocks when building infrastructure: vague and undefined roles and responsibilities, lack of accountability or incentives for performance, lack of management talent to achieve growth goals, lack of financial controls to monitor current and projected financial performance, and ignoring or underestimating technology as a strategic tool.

Chapter 8. Staying One Step Ahead

Once you understand the long-term implications of material covered in this book, you should take actions to follow through on the steps recommended in the Growth Strategy Analysis. This chapter lists a series of resources from *Inc.*, including a Web site and other forms of connection, that will support you as you take action to apply the book's ideas and tools.

SUCCESS IS UP TO YOU

All business growth experts agree on one thing: A company's future success or failure is *always within management's control.* Business failure is rarely the result of a lack of information, talent, or technology. Rather, it is the result of poor judgment at the top. It is safe to say that as a business leader, you are ultimately responsible for your organization's future destiny. This may inspire some, and invoke fear in others. But the fact is that *you* have the ability to control your company's behavior so that it can grow effectively, and achieve the goals you desire. Yet as every CEO of a growing company knows, guidance is often lacking on how that success can be achieved in an environment of constant change.

One of the objectives of *Inc.* magazine is to create a community of company builders who can share their experiences and realize they are not alone. Throughout this book, the experiences of thousands of growing companies provide the backdrop for viewing your own company, and will help you gain perspective on your situation.

Often clarity in business comes not from having all the answers, but from *knowing the right questions to ask.* This book will give you the right questions to ask yourself and your employees to assess your organization's growth potential. And it gives you the tools to do something about it. If you make the effort, you will create an extraordinary future for yourself and your company.

ACKNOWLEDGMENTS

THANKS TO JOHN BELL AT PERSEUS BOOKS FOR BEING the first person to get behind this project. Also to Nick Philipson— I've always appreciated your enthusiastic support.

I am especially grateful to the commitment of the staff at *Inc.* Business Resources, particularly Jan Spiro and Brad Ketchum, Jr. Jan kept the project on track, managing the various twists and turns with both genuine care and a sound business sensibility. And Brad Ketchum's laser-like editorial insights were absolutely superior. Thanks also to those at *Inc.* who have supported my work over the years: Bob LaPointe, Linda Burton, and Bernie Goldhirsh.

I would also like to give a special note of gratitude to all the consultants who have worked with me at various points during the seven years that I was running *Inc.*'s Growth Strategy Consulting Group. They are: Katherine Catlin (who first introduced me to the concept of the S-curve and how it connected to growing companies), Keith Bailey and Karen Dunn of Sterling Consulting, Richard Russakoff, Ken Cook, Kevin Wiese, Julian Smerkovitz, and Matt Seward and Richard Zahn of Innovative Partners. Each person has taught me invaluable lessons about the consulting business, acting as my mentors while I was building the Growth Strategy Consulting Group. Each one has contributed uniquely to this book in some fashion or another, and without them the development of the concepts presented in *The Next Level* would not have been possible. It's a great thing to find professional colleagues who are not only respected as being the best in the business, but can also be counted as friends. My deepest thanks to each of you.

CHAPTER ONE

The Growth Curve

FOR THE PAST 20 YEARS, *INC.* MAGAZINE HAS REPORTED the stories of thousands of successful companies. Although each company is unique in terms of its products, services, and technologies, the stories reveal a common theme: *Every growth company reaches critical transitional points that require fundamental changes.* Sooner or later it happens. Whatever brought success in the past—the structures, strategies, and systems—no longer works as well. If an organization cannot recognize its need to change, it struggles with the same problems over and over again. Instead of experiencing new levels of growth and success, it stalls, flounders, or fails. This experience of hitting an invisible barrier after a period of steady growth is a collective thread that binds growth companies together.

Traditional concepts of growth offer little guidance on how to deal with such barriers. Wall Street–driven firms have long preached that sales and earnings performance should resemble a line that begins on the bottom left of the chart and then follows a straight path to the opposite top right corner. Although the quantitative aspects of business growth may follow such a path, the dynamics of growth as experienced from management's point of view are very different (see graph on next page).

The graphic representation of a straight line assumes that managing growth involves simply doing more of the same, but on a bigger scale. It looks so easy! Just set your sales goals, and hit them! Just sell more, and you are sure to grow. Real-world experience reveals that this is not the case.

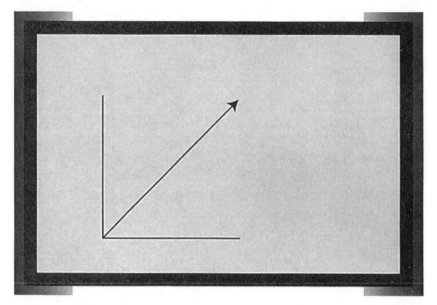

Inc. magazine's editor-in-chief, George Gendron, likes to use this analogy for the experience of business growth: Managing growth, he says, is similar to playing a video game—once you master the first level, you get bumped to the next, more difficult, level, where you meet a more complicated array of variables. The same is true in business. Getting bigger is not just a matter of doing more of the same thing—it involves mastering a whole new set of complex variables in order to succeed.

Successful growth requires mastering such issues as financial needs, human resources, technological alterations, competitive challenges, and market demands that were not present when the company was smaller. For a growing company, the world is no longer as simple as just selling more.

THE S-CURVE

One model for growth that has been utilized for decades by scientists and business theorists alike is called the S-curve. Although not a new concept, the S-curve is extremely effective in describing the turbulent patterns that occur as a company grows.

The point of the S-curve is that growth is cyclical. Each period of growth is inevitably interrupted by a break, causing one curve to end and another to begin. The factors that contributed to a company's ascending the first curve are not the same ones required for it to climb the second curve. The first curve, if continued, will eventually lead to stagnation, deterioration, and ultimately death. Regardless of the amount of effort applied, the path of the original curve eventually peaks and declines. One cannot get from one level to the next by continuing on the same path. In order to survive, and to grow, one must *begin a new growth curve*. This requires breaking away from the patterns that contributed to the first curve, and generating *new* actions, adaptations, and behaviors. A transformation, or reinvention, is necessary for survival.

The demise of one curve, the growth of the next, and the void in between are focal points for tremendous personal and company stress. The experience of organizational chaos, the sense of feeling overwhelmed, the exhilarating rush driven by adrenaline are all natural reactions to finding oneself in midflight over the abyss between the first and second curves. The S-curve aptly explains the turmoil of fast-growth companies.

Three stages characterize a business's journey from its inception to being a fully developed organization: start-up, rapid growth, and transition (see graph, below).

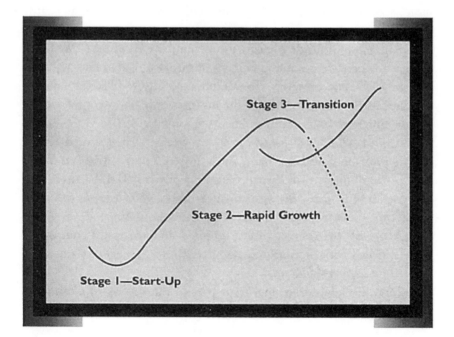

Stage 1: Start-up

This stage represents the earliest phase in entrepreneurial ventures, when ideas turn from dreams into reality. As anyone who has created a business knows, the start-up period is driven solely by the imperative of making sales. Getting the next customer is all that matters. Regardless of how great the product or service, how wonderful the business idea is, and how much the entrepreneur believes the market needs this product or service, without enough sales the business will never get off the ground.

At Stage 1, entrepreneurs are consumed by the business. Constrained by limited financial resources, they utilize creativity and an "on the edge" spirit to drive their companies to success. Their tendency toward risk taking, their unquenchable faith in what they're doing, and their sheer persistence push these new ventures forward. "When you're in the start-up mode, everything is compressed," says Steve Bostic, former CEO of American Photo Group. "You make the wrong move, and you can go right out. It clearly is the high wire."

During this time, everything is new and untested. Precedents are lacking. Gut instinct and intuition are the rule for making decisions. The entrepreneur's approach is a chaotic, disorganized search of the marketplace to find opportunities and customers. He or she is figuring out what works and what doesn't work—how to market, sell, and promote, whom to market to. Experimentation and discovery are daily occurrences.

A gung-ho attitude prevails throughout the company: "We'll do whatever it takes to get the next piece of business. Otherwise, we may not survive!" For example, Tom Golisano, CEO of $700 million Paychex, recalls the early days of the business. His start-up goal was to attract 300 new small-business clients for his payroll services. Tom's start-up cash of $3,000 lasted about six weeks. "Then I used credit cards, I took out consumer loans, and I fudged. I sent out several thousand pieces of direct mail. My nieces and nephews licked the envelopes at night." It took nearly five years to attract those 300 customers, during which time Golisano went without a paycheck himself.

Many of this century's most admired and successful companies were launched with precious few resources. Instead, ingenuity gets substituted for capital resources.

Ingenuity played an important part in the success of Corporate Resource Development (CRD), an *Inc.* 500 company specializing in training and consulting. Max Carey, CRD's founder, recalls that during the desperate early days of his business, after the credit cards were exhausted, the cash was short, and the family car was repossessed, he received a call from the state's department of taxation. "Do you folks do training with taxation offices?" the caller asked. "Sure," Carey replied and without missing a beat said, "Let me transfer you to that department." He put the caller on hold and screamed over to his partner at the next desk, "This is a lead! The state tax office. Pick up the phone and answer, 'Tax Department'!" His partner followed Carey's instructions. CRD landed a much-desired contract, and the money it badly needed to keep going. CRD is now a flourishing $5 million company. Carey's desperation drove his creative embellishment.

During Stage 1, the business can be extremely agile and flexible. Structures and systems are loose, if they exist at all. Employees have no job description, doing what needs to be done, and that changes daily. Neal DeAngelo is the owner of DeAngelo Brothers, Inc., a weed-control service for railroads and utilities in Hazelton, Pennsylvania, (estimated 1997 revenues: $12 million). DeAngelo says of his early days in the business: "You hire people to do one thing, but if they can also do two other things, you tend to have them do all three instead of hiring additional staff or contracting out." It is this flexibility and lack of formal policy for "how things are supposed to be done" that allows the entrepreneurial start-up to achieve some pretty amazing feats.

Formal planning during this stage is irrelevant. In fact, many entrepreneurs who start with a business plan toss it away once their businesses are in operation. New opportunities often emerge that were never imagined in the original plan. An example is Mapinfo Corp. in Troy, New York, which provides desktop mapping software for personal computers (estimated 1997 revenues: $50 million). The company's initial concept was developing sensors in a car's wheels that could locate the car's position on an electronic street. After several months of work, the partners scrapped the idea. They then went to banks, police and fire departments, government agencies, insurance companies, and other companies that dealt with the characteristics of geography. The partners asked, "What should our software do for you to be interested in it?" The consensus: It should retrieve demographic statistics from a database and draw them on a map. This response led the partners to produce the world's first mapping software to run on a desktop computer. Now a public company with a broad product line, Mapinfo still relies on customers to dictate new directions.

During the start-up phase, the entrepreneur faces constant pressure to reshape his business concept as he bumps up against the real world. Opportunities must be seized upon in a moment's notice in order for the business to turn the next corner. The stakes are high. The adrenaline surges. Every door is pounded on until it is either opened or slammed. Winning is everything. These are the guts and glory of Stage 1.

Stage 2: Rapid Growth

Stage 2 occurs when a business's sales and customer base reaches critical mass. The company has found a niche, a market, and a formula for success. There is no longer a mad rush to find new business week to week. The sense of desperation is not as prevalent—the business is off the high wire and is resting on solid ground. All the entrepreneur's efforts and persistence—chasing leads, selling new customers, outsmarting competitors, and pulling the business together on a shoestring—have paid off. No doubt, some good luck and timing have also played a part in getting to this stage. However it happened, the business is now growing.

Kevin Clark, president of Edge Software Services in Warrenton, Virginia, remembers the exact moment when he realized his band of software engineers had actually turned into something more than a few guys doing technical work. "It was like waking up one day after three years of consulting with my partners, and I thought 'Wow! We have a business on our hands!'"

Edge provides software consulting services to banks and financial institutions. The business began in January of 1993, when the five partners left their technical positions in a bank and decided to hit the road on their own. Because of their reputation and connections in the industry, business rolled in at a steady pace. Additional consultants were hired to help keep up with the momentum. Soon Edge had 15 employees instead of just the five partners. One day, Clark looked around at his company and employees and it hit him: This business was here to stay.

With that realization came an enormous feeling of responsibility. "By trade, we are all technicians. We were just out there winging it. But when I saw 15 people and more coming on board soon, I started to feel that we had to be more responsible for building the business." In the fall of 1996, Clark knew his business needed more proactive leadership, and he decided to stop consulting so that he could focus on developing the company's operational infrastructure.

During Stage 2, successful business patterns replace ad hoc experimentation. The business is now intent on understanding how those patterns are developing. What are you are actually selling? Who is buying? How are you delivering the product or service? How can you streamline operations and improve efficiencies?

Internal Systems

Whereas new sales are the top priority in Stage 1, the critical issue in Stage 2 is a company's ability to organize. During this stage, the pendulum swings from a purely sales-driven attitude to a focus on the business's internal workings. Improvements in management, stability, and structure are necessary in order for the rapid-growth company to capitalize on new growth and revenue opportunities. As the number of customers, employees, and transactions increases along with the organization's complexity, the business must find out what works best operationally, and then create the systems to replicate these activities. This in turn establishes the efficiencies required to manage the sheer volume of activity and accommodate additional growth.

Where getting new business is the lifeblood of the Stage 1 company, the most important aim of Stage 2 is developing the ability to consistently satisfy those customers. If the business doesn't institute operational systems and efficiencies, it will develop problems with customer delivery, quality, and service. The danger then exists that dissatisfied customers will not put up with poor performance and will move on to a competitor.

As Kevin Clark of Edge Software turned his attention to his company's internal workings, he discovered that he had a bigger job ahead of him than anticipated. "I went to a conference for CEOs of growing companies and I came back realizing all the things we weren't doing." He decided that Edge's first priority was getting its financing in order. "Our clients had always paid well, so we didn't really notice cash-flow problems until we had a payroll to deal with." But with 15 employees—which became 25 within a few months—Clark knew that he needed additional financial backing. He turned to a financial consultant to assist him in lining up the financing he needed from a local bank.

The second priority was what Clark calls the "back office." Since all consulting projects take place at client locations, everyone was traveling most of the time, except for two employees running the office. Clark didn't have a clue about what they did. "I remember talking with my business adviser," Clark recalls. "He asked me how many hours per week I thought those two office staff were working. I remembered one started as part time to help the other. 'Maybe they're up to 40 hours each?' I said." When Clark actually asked them, he discovered they were both working between 50 and 60 hours a week. "I had no idea how much work they were doing just trying to keep up with the growth from the previous year," Clark explains. "And knowing that we were going to double in size in the coming year, I had to deal with that area fast."

In the year and a half that followed, Clark diligently laid the groundwork for Edge's continued growth. One partner became chief operating officer. Together, he and Clark are building the systems and streamlining daily operations. They've invested in the software and hardware to set up financial controls and to automate the financial management, including payroll, general ledger, and management reporting. They have also created a company policy manual. Next they will be focusing on the human resources function. This will help with the hiring and retention of consultants.

Clark understands that the company must focus on internal systems in order to grow and get to the next level. "This and next year we have huge opportunities for growth. Our biggest concern has been to make sure that we are positioned to handle it."

During the transition from start-up to rapid growth, business owners recognize that they can no longer do everything and begin to delegate responsibilities. They hire or promote managers who are responsible for specific tasks or functions. Managers focus on how to make their departments run as efficiently as possible. Breakdowns that managers encounter are treated as lessons learned: Find the origin of the problem and fix it so that it doesn't happen again.

Functional departments emerge. Now there is a sales manager and soon a sales department; or there is a controller and then an accounting department. An office manager, service manager, or plant manager is hired.

Stage 2 is generally an exciting period of growth for an entrepreneur. Success breeds success—the more the company improves, the more it grows. The key challenge is to keep up with the growth opportunities while hiring more people and putting the appropriate systems and structures in place.

Implosion

Some companies never make it beyond Stage 2 because they can't shift from a focus on sales to one on operations. These are the companies you may hear about that "grow too fast." They simply implode because appropriate attention isn't given to internal issues. Instead, they get caught up in the excitement and energy of selling more—because they believe that more sales means more success. That is true only if operations get equal attention; but if operations continue to be ignored then more sales will only lead to an inevitable crisis.

Three-Five Systems, Inc., a maker of cellular telephone display panels in Tempe, Arizona, illustrates how sales can become a trap. Three-Five saw its profits rise tenfold in two years, and landed twice on the *Forbes* 200 Best Small Companies list. Three-Five went public in 1990 at 75 cents a share. During 1994, Three-Five's stock topped $50, split 2 for 1, then reached $50 again. A $1,000 investment in the shares returned $133,000 in four years.

Unfortunately, investors never noticed that Three-Five was highly vulnerable: It depended on Motorola for 85 percent of its sales. In early 1996, Motorola changed its product line. Consequently it needed far fewer panels from Three-Five. That year, revenues dropped 34 percent (from $92 million to $62 million), inventory write-offs wiped out profits, and the stock fell to $8.75.

David R. Buchanan, Three-Five's president and CEO, recalled that winning Motorola's order was a terrific coup for a young company, but that it carried risks. "We knew that we had to diversify," Buchanan said. "But we couldn't build infrastructure fast enough to expand beyond Motorola. We couldn't hire people fast enough. What else could we do? I couldn't give away sales."

Sales-oriented entrepreneurs must become systems-minded leaders during Stage 2 growth so they can give more attention to operational issues.

Bursting at the Seams

Action Sports (name has been disguised to protect confidentiality), a sporting goods distributor in Los Angeles, had grown to $50 million in sales, but found itself "bursting at the seams" because it lacked the infrastructure to accommodate growth.

Don Robby, who started this family-run business more than 40 years ago, was a vibrant, charismatic owner who developed a solid reputation in the industry and a loyal base of customers. His knowledge, contacts, decision-making ability, and understanding of the clothing industry enabled Action Sports to experience consistent growth. But Robby neglected to establish the systems and structures that would allow the business to function in his absence.

As Robby aged, he developed a degenerative disease that slowly chipped away at his physical abilities. Unable to manage the company full time, Robby tapped his son Bob to head operations, and his son Harry to do selling. Although inexperienced—both had never worked outside of the firm and had followed orders from their father—they took active leadership roles.

During the early phase of this transfer of power, Robby still kept an eye on things. But as his disease worsened, he lost his ability to speak and to control his muscles. Robby rarely advised his sons on daily business issues. Yet the company boomed. Harry sold with a vengeance. Bob managed operations using his father's technique of running the business out of his head.

Three years from the time of the brothers' ascent, Action Sports had become like a pressure cooker without a release valve—it was ready to explode. Its infrastructure was nonexistent. No computer systems tracked financial information and inventory. Employees lacked job titles. Customer service was poor. The work environment was chaotic, with redundancies, bottlenecks, and inefficiencies ruling the day. No standards were issued for how to conduct the business—every question or decision had to be run through Bob and Harry. No one took responsibility for the recurring mistakes.

The business, now with 50 employees, peaked at $50 million in sales. With the poor quality of operations the business could not physically handle any more orders, so Harry stopped selling. Bob and Harry were burned out by all the problems. The family decided to sell the company to a large, publicly traded competitor. It was best for the family and for the business. Bob and Harry lacked the leadership skills and the experience to establish an effective infrastructure and they knew it.

During the selling process, the prospective owners discovered that $6 million in inventory had been sitting in a warehouse for years. Also they uncovered that a key manager had embezzled hundreds of thousands of dollars. No one had noticed because of the lack of financial controls.

Crisis Driven

Many companies, particularly fast-growing ones like Action Sports, learn the importance of infrastructure only *because* of a crisis. Often the crisis is financial, as a result of poor accounting and financial systems. Sales pour in, but the money isn't tracked. This has caused the death of many promising businesses.

Many entrepreneurs have little interest in financial management. Most lack formal training in business or finance, and must rely on others to supply the information. Says Claudia Post, CEO of Diamond Courier Service in Philadelphia, Pennsylvania, "I was busy having a great time selling. Cash flow? Profit before taxes? I didn't know how to figure out any of that stuff." Claudia was just a selling machine. As a result of her neglect, her then $3.5 million company began experiencing chronic cash-flow problems. In addition, the lack of operating systems created a vacuum of information.

Fortunately for Diamond Courier, Claudia found a financial adviser who helped her build the necessary management tools, and then assisted her in making some tough decisions. In the last two years, the unprofitable venture has become a profitable business, revenue per job has more than doubled, and the business is in the black.

Rising Without Chaos

The Saint Louis Bread Company illustrates the right way to grow through Stage 2. In 1997 the company's revenues were $70.3 million, up from $17.8 million only five years before. The company enjoyed initial success because of the strength of its original concept: 11 bread varieties, and with more than 25 types of muffins, Danish pastries, and croissants are baked the day they are sold. The old-time bakery counter brings in the customers, while the soup and sandwich counter does the volume.

As Saint Louis Bread launched its first five stores from 1989 to 1990, Ken Rosenthal, then president, consulted with Stern Fixture, a local equipment-supply company, to find more efficient ways to design their deli operations. "Sandwiches were something they were doing as an adjunct to their bread business," says Mal Dardick, a designer and the chairman of Stern, "and we said, 'What are you going to do if everybody likes the product and they all come at once and you can't turn the food out quickly and cleanly?' We helped them think about better layouts for mass production."

Through small and steady backroom improvements, the company primed itself for controlled expansion. Rosenthal and his management team combined aggressive development with cautious calculation, and a sense of what aspect of operations should take priority each step of the way.

By mid-1992, Saint Louis Bread had 10 stores running with another 7 slated to open that fall and winter. Don Berger, one of Rosenthal's two partners, remembers that the pace had begun to feel frantic. "It was like running so hard that you can't breathe, but you have to keep running." Things weren't out of control yet, but it was getting harder for the three partners to visit all the stores as often as they wanted. In addition, the margins were a little soggy. 1990 sales were $2.8 million, with a profit margin of just 1.4 percent, and 1991 sales were $5.8 million, with margins at 1.7 percent (Au Bon Pain, a publicly traded café chain based in New England, had margins of 5.5 percent). Employee turnover was another trouble spot, replicating the industry average of about 100 percent annually, which they had always tried to beat.

At this point, the partners decided to do something that seems unthinkable to most entrepreneurs: stop growing. "It was time to take a breath, sit back, and make sure that everybody was thinking about the same thing and that we all had the same vision," says Rosenthal. After planning in three- to six-month spurts, they agreed to plan for the next one to two years.

"The opportunistic approach this company had taken," says Richard Happel, the former chief financial officer, "wouldn't work anymore. Everyone here knows we have a window of opportunity, and we're anxious to capitalize on it. But the owners understood, above all else, that without the substructure, the superstructure would never hold. We reached the point where the controls and the information systems we had in place were woefully inadequate for a larger organization. And if we didn't stop soon, we were going to reach the point where we had total chaos."

To help in the planning process, the partners brought in a team of outside facilitators to lead 10 managers through a two-month, 50-hour evaluation of the business. During this exercise, the managers reached agreement on how many stores there should be in the chain, where those stores would be located, and what sales volume they wanted to plan for each store. They then wrote out detailed schedules for the steps needed to reach these targets. Two documents emerged from this evaluation: a business plan and a calendar of actions to meet strategic goals.

With this plan in place, the partners began investing in the company's infrastructure. They bought state-of-the-art point-of-purchase registers (at $30,000 a pop), which allow Saint Louis Bread to track business elements better, including sales per hour, sales per stock-keeping unit (SKU), sales by stores, and labor per dollar generated. At the bakery, new equipment began automating processes on the line, enabling the same number of people to make more product.

In addition to these internal steps, Saint Louis Bread improved its relationships with its suppliers. It provided them with a seven-page synopsis of the strategic plan to keep them up-to-date on the company's goals. "Most food-service people are not organized at all," says Paul Landsbaum, president and owner of Stern Fixture, which supplies Saint Louis Bread with its furniture, fixtures, and equipment. He notes,"What makes Saint Louis Bread different is that it approached the food-service business from the viewpoint of a retailer. The company excels at displaying its wares and attracting the sale. And because it gives us projections, we can go out to our suppliers and strike volume deals on Saint Louis Bread's behalf."

Rosenthal now believes that because they stopped and put in place these changes, the company is in the position to take on the next stage of growth with more stability and structure.

Stage 3: Transition

As companies build their operational infrastructures and increase sales during Stage 2, they enjoy a period of steady growth. Then something strange happens: The formulas that worked so well are no longer effective. The strategies that brought the company to its current level of success are no longer achieving the same results. Carefully planned and executed internal infrastructures begin to bog down. The organizational structure that worked fine when the company was smaller is not appropriate anymore. *All of the fundamental assumptions about the business are now in question.* The business has hit Stage 3.

At this point one of three things happens: The business plateaus, reaching its own internal limitations to growth; or the company slowly deteriorates as it clings to the old formulas, while the outside world continues to change; or the company experiences a breakthrough by redefining its business strategies, structures, or systems.

Stage 3 represents an inevitable crossroads for every growing organization. To continue growth, the organization must break from past patterns of success by either embracing new behaviors and actions, or by reconfiguring old patterns. If this stage is managed well, the company begins a new cycle on the growth curve; if it is not managed well, then the company stagnates or declines.

Gadi Rosenfeld of Legal Information Technology, in New York City, was an *Inc.* 500 company CEO who grew his business by redefining what business he was in. He and his partner, Dan Court, observed the explosion of office computer local-area networks (LANs). So in 1989 they started a business to install LANs in law offices. But they were too late. No sooner had Rosenfeld and Court entered the market, than a flood of competitors followed. This intense competition damaged profitability. "Margins kept on slipping," Rosenfeld remembers. "This business was becoming a commodity."

Instead of toughing it out, Rosenfeld and Court sought to make their company distinctive by scanning legal documents into a computer and then storing the information on CD-ROMs. To date, Legal Information Technology has grown from sales of $120,000 in 1989 to $30 million in 1997. Although the company still does systems integration and LAN installations, Rosenfeld estimates that nearly all of its business now consists of scanning information onto CD-ROMs and coding it. By changing course, Rosenfeld "jumped the curve" to a new field where the profit potential was greater and the competition less intense.

External variables often play a significant role in hurling an unsuspecting company into Stage 3. New competitors, shifting market conditions, the introduction of new technology, changing customer demands and preferences—all can bring on a break in the growth curve. In order to grow and compete, a company must either change its strategies and patterns of success from the past, or deal with the consequences.

Failing to Change

Prism Group's demise illustrates what happens to a company if it cannot alter its old formula for success to keep up with new market conditions. Prism Group, a software duplicator and distributor, had grown to sales of $7 million in 1991. Prism's CEO K. C. Aly, had visions of transforming the business into a national service company with earnings as high as $125 million. But the software manufacturing and distribution business became intensely competitive. As the software industry grew, publishers sought to increase their profit margins by putting pressure on companies like Prism. Simultaneously, changes in media platforms eroded profit margins. So Aly devised a plan. He would acquire several regional suppliers and transform Prism Group into a service company. It would take orders from customers and distribute software electronically, taking its cut from each transaction. This strategy, he reasoned, would shield Prism from the costs wreaked by future changes in media platforms. Prism's board of directors didn't agree. The board viewed Prism as a manufacturing business that should focus on increasing sales and streamlining operations. In 1993, the board ousted Aly.

As software companies switched to CD-ROM, Prism's business steadily declined. Prism Group had acquired another software manufacturer and formed a subsidiary, Prism Software Production. Nearly half of the subsidiary's $21 million in sales came from three customers, the largest of whom dropped Prism Group for a competitor.

Trying to catch a second wind, Prism's board in May 1995 brought back Aly as CEO. They wanted him to pursue a strategy close to his original plan. After some debt consolidation by Aly, the company's performance improved—its net loss was reduced from more than $5 million in 1994 to about $860,000 in 1995. But Prism's considerable debt and a slow market transition torpedoed the recovery. The company closed its doors in 1996. They missed the window of opportunity for making the critical transformation required to begin a new growth curve.

Internal Factors

Internal variables can also play a part in bringing a company into Stage 3. Usually they involve organizational and operational issues, such as lack of management depth, or limitations on existing equipment or information systems that cannot handle the increased volume of business transactions.

Organizational structure is a good example. Many companies, as they experience the rapid growth of Stage 2 will cope by finding any warm body they can to fill new positions. As the business owner begins to delegate, he or she will typically promote people internally rather than hire professionals from the outside. The two reasons for this are: (1) that they can't afford professional managers, and (2) that it is easier and more convenient to promote from within. Sometimes home-grown managers work out. More often, a company's growth will outpace these managers' skills and experience. They simply don't have the experience to draw on in making appropriate management decisions. For instance, when a company is small, a bookkeeper is sufficient for tracking historical accounting records and working with budgets and tax reports. But when a company is ready for serious financing, or its strategies involve a merger or acquisition, no amount of on-the-job training will prepare that same bookkeeper for the sophisticated negotiations, valuations, and financial projections that will be needed. The company's financial position is one of many functions within the organization where professional management may be necessary for a company to enter the next growth curve. Others include marketing, operations, and human resources.

Bill Liebegott, president of Hi-Tech Hose in Newburyport, Massachusetts, says that his company has outgrown his existing team of managers. With $8 million in sales in 1997, the company was still profitable, but the level of sophistication it was reaching was far surpassing the abilities of many employees. "Our people were clearly unable to get the company to the next level. We noticed that we were dealing with the same issues over and over again," he reflects. "I realized that in order to keep growing and have some fun again, I had to get the right team of people on board." For Hi-Tech Hose that meant hiring professionals with skills and experiences that didn't exist in the business before. Bill and his wife Max, the vice president of sales, now wanted to surround themselves with the right people who would help them achieve their vision for growth. That also meant making some tough calls regarding existing staff. Bill comments, "It's not the people you fire that give you the problems. It's the people you don't fire."

Nonprofits: The American Council on Exercise

Sheryl Marks Brown was a little nervous. She was about to make a presentation to her employees that was downright depressing. She rehearsed her opening lines. *"This organization will die a slow death unless we do something now."* How would employees react to that doom-and-gloom message? *"Our standards for performance aren't good enough anymore."* When they heard this, would they think the organization is going down the chute? *"We cannot continue to run this business the same as we always have in the past."*

It's not as if her nonprofit organization, American Council on Exercise (ACE), in San Diego, California, was experiencing any trouble. It was actually quite successful. ACE provides certification programs to aerobics and exercise instructors who work in fitness clubs, as well as to personal trainers. With the boom in the fitness industry over the past two decades, ACE has enjoyed steady growth, and the ACE "seal of approval" commands international recognition. For the fitness instructor who has little or no formal training, ACE certification provides a professional credential and a certain cachet. That, in turn, increases respect and confidence among the exercising public.

As its certification programs flourished, ACE began reviewing exercise equipment much as *Consumer Reports* does. Business was good—ACE received between 25,000 and 35,000 calls per month from people who looked to ACE for instruction certification and consumer information. Employees felt terrific about the organization's success. But in spite of all of this, Brown was uncomfortable. She had a nagging sense that the wave ACE had been riding was going to crash.

There was justification for Brown's intuition. For one thing, the market seemed to have peaked. ACE had hit $5 million in annual revenues, and had hovered there for several years. But that was a problem that could be worked out, Brown reasoned. They had plenty of good ideas for new products and services.

The more worrisome threat came from ACE's chief competitor, the American College of Sports Medicine (ACSM). For the most part, ACE and ACSM had left each other alone. ACE had focused on the mainstream fitness and club market, and ACSM had concentrated on hospitals and cardiac rehabilitation programs. However, ACSM's new executive director had decided to aggressively go after the fitness club market.

ACSM had the medical and academic community's support and the clout that came with it. For the first time, ACE's world was threatened.

"It's hard to forecast doom when things look and feel so good," Brown says. "After being so proud of our accomplishments over the past 10 years, it was quite a challenge to figure how to shake people up without scaring them away. I really wanted to activate and motivate people without making them feel that the world was crashing in around them."

Her carefully worded presentation to her employees that day got the message across: We've been successful in the past, but that doesn't mean we can be complacent. Plenty of profit-driven companies such as Digital Equipment, RCA, and Westinghouse couldn't change and stay ahead of the competition. Since that meeting in 1997, Sheryl has been working methodically with her employees and her board to think through ACE's challenges carefully.

Besides the ACSM threat, internal issues needed to be addressed. With up to 35,000 calls a month, ACE needed more sophis-ticated technology to generate customer data. This data could help provide ideas for new strategies for growth. So ACE has installed the hardware and software that will take it to the next level.

Brown now spends much of her time on strategic decisions— the type that could have a longer-term impact on the organization's visibility, growth, and success. For instance, one of ACE's strategies for growth involves partnering with corporations to increase its reach, image, and brand-name recognition.

In addition, Brown is focusing on developing her board of direc-tors. "I used to have people from the fitness industry, and thought that was enough," she says. "Now I'm inviting more businesspeople from the corporate community to serve on our board. They may know nothing about fitness, but if they know business and have connections in the corporate world, they will help us achieve our long-term strategies."

SYMPTOMS OF TRANSITION

Regardless of whether the cause is internal or external factors, every growing company eventually reaches Stage 3. Several symptoms indicate when a company has reached the transition stage.

One symptom is a breakdown of internal communications. This is often due to the confusion and chaos caused by internal and external changes. For example, when functional departments emerge during Stage 2, their focus is often on improving their individual efficiencies and systems to accommodate additional growth. And that is exactly what the company needs during rapid growth. But as the company continues to grow and change, those efforts can result in isolation and territorialism. Instead of working together toward common company goals, departments end up only interested in maintaining their own agendas.

Another symptom of transition is that customers are no longer a priority. In fact, they are taken for granted. Instead, the company's energy is caught up in internal politics and management issues. This shift toward an internal focus can become quite problematic, and extremely difficult to overcome. Forgetting about the customer has been the demise of many growth companies. A recent survey released by Price Waterhouse provides a case in point, and is a warning bell for all communications companies. They found that 41 percent of pager, cellular phones, and Internet customers are irritated by the lack of customer service demonstrated by the companies in these hot industries. One possible result of this decline in service, is that the growth rate for paging services has slowed to 21 percent in 1997, down from 31 percent in 1995. And the second-largest paging carrier, MobileMedia Corp, has filed for bankruptcy protection. The reason, according to Alex, Brown analyst Brian Coleman, is that "the focus in the paging industry has been on growth, consolidation and developing new services. As a result of this, customer-base maintenance has not been first and foremost."

A third symptom of the transition stage is a change in the CEO's clarity and passion for the future. Many entrepreneurs who reach Stage 3 have driven their company from virtually nothing to their current level of success. They then realize that their original vision for their company has already been reached. So now they ask, "What's next?

Where do we go from here?" The original goal was to get beyond a hand-to-mouth existence; the next goal was to make a little profit at the end of the year. Now the entrepreneur goes into his office building and *doesn't even know the names of the staff* anymore! The stakes are much higher. Many more employees' livelihoods are on the line. Feelings of uncertainty and fear replace the passion and drive that fueled the early stages of business growth.

As the company in Stage 3 faces fundamental change, it often resorts to working harder at old routines. Managers and employees put in longer hours, try to sell more, and attempt to squeeze every improvement possible out of the existing organization. Unfortunately, these increased efforts only result in incremental improvements rather than marked progress in business performance. Overall, the Stage 3 company is more reactive than proactive. Managers feel out of control, constantly reacting to the marketplace as well as organizational situations.

CLIMBING TO THE NEXT LEVEL OF GROWTH

The S-curve model captures a company's experience of cycles of turbulence and acceleration. The periods of disturbance, confusion, and chaos during Stage 3 are normal signs of new or emerging business conditions. They force a company to break from the familiar patterns of the past and take on the new, yet uncertain, future. This stage of chaos represents a crossroads—new actions, behaviors, and patterns must emerge for the organization to survive. Tremendous conflict and resistance usually ensue. If they are not overcome, the company stagnates and eventually declines.

For owners and employees alike, this stage involves taking chances and launching into new, unfamiliar territory. It means leaving behind the ways that employees are comfortable with and have worked hard to figure out, and that have contributed enormously to their success. All must be questioned, which invariably brings pain and discomfort. But it is a necessary part of growth. A company cannot grow while staying the same. It is literally impossible. So the upheavals experienced by a company are lessons from the outside world that must be received and learned.

Some business owners find this difficult to accept. They have developed a recipe for success, one that was discovered during those treacherous days of Stage 1 and then fine-tuned during Stage 2. This recipe has brought ever-escalating salaries and bonuses, and peer and even industry recognition. These experiences validate their recipe for success and reinforce how they think the world works. Then comes Stage 3.

Many companies cannot take on new ideas, risks, and strategies until they are aware of, and dissatisfied with, the misalignment between prior success and future challenges. In *Competing for the Future*, business consultants Gary Hamel and C. K. Prahald point out that "the future is not an extrapolation of the past." They illustrate this concept using Les Aberthal, the CEO of Electronic Data Systems (EDS). In 1992, Aberthal was preparing to address a worldwide gathering of EDS executives. EDS has been extremely successful up to then. Aberthal worried that the executives were feeling too comfortable with the success. So he asked an assistant to research the *Fortune* 500 list from 20 years before and find out how many of those firms still existed in 1991. The assistant reported back that only 40 percent of the 1971 *Fortune* 500 firms remained. Aberthal attributed their failure to two management missteps: an inability to escape the past, and an incompetence to create the future.

When a company enjoys abundant resources and wealth and when employees are generally content with their work, the company becomes vulnerable because the rules of the game will inevitably change. These vanished *Fortune* 500 companies most likely did not even notice the changes until it was too late. Even if they did, they found it impossible to alter the course to meet the demands of a new environment because they did not have the capacity to change.

Entrepreneurial companies are just as vulnerable to being caught up in their own agendas, to becoming oblivious to the changing demands around them, and to becoming paralyzed, unable to take corrective action. Although small companies have fewer people and less bureaucracy to weigh them down when they want to change, they also have limited resources. The marketplace grants no mercy, and these companies have little financial slack to make up for lost time or missed opportunities. Business leaders must continually be prepared to challenge the successes of the past so they can take on future opportunities.

THE KEY TO BREAKTHROUGH GROWTH: JUMPING THE CURVE

An organization's ability to make the leap from one curve to the next is the key to long-term growth. Once your company has made it through the first growth cycle, it's going to experience the cycle all over again. You face all the same challenges, just at another level. Some companies may experience the full cycle over a long period of time, perhaps years or decades. Other companies can experience the S-curve several times in rapid succession within a very short period. There are no time frames for this process. Those companies that are prepared for and skilled at "jumping the curve" will progressively grow from one level to the next. Those that can't will always struggle and feel they are standing on the edge of corporate catastrophe.

The ability to navigate from one curve to the next determines your company's growth potential. Jumping the curve does not stem from generating more sales, installing a new computer system, or developing a quality-improvement program. Although each of these is important, none on its own will lead to a company's capability to grow over the long term. So what does it take to achieve breakthrough growth? What is the secret? There are five Growth Drivers that *must* be in place in order for an organization to grow effectively for the long term:

- Market intelligence
- Strategic leadership
- Clarity of purpose
- Strategic planning
- Internal infrastructure

These are the fundamental business and management practices that most directly affect your company's growth over the long term. Each of these is described in the following chapters, and exercises and tools are presented to use for executing the Growth Drivers appropriately in your own company. But before reading about the Growth Drivers, here's a 12-point quiz that can help you determine your company's current stage of growth.

ANALYSIS: AT WHAT STAGE OF GROWTH IS YOUR COMPANY?

Circle the statement that most applies to your company.

1. STRATEGIES FOR GROWTH

A. Since our niche has not yet been established, we are exploring several markets to determine our most effective growth strategy.

B. We have tapped into a market that is expanding, and we are riding the wave of demand as we grow.

C. With a very competitive and mature market, we constantly are looking for new strategies to grow.

D. The market is declining and we have lost many windows of opportunity; we are trying to gain market share by increasing our sales efforts.

2. MARKET CONDITIONS

A. The market is brand-new, and the technology/service we provide is also relatively new.

B. The market is growing at a strong pace, and opportunities abound.

C. The market has stabilized, and growth opportunities will soon peak.

D. The market is declining and is being replaced with new concepts/technologies.

3. COMPETITIVE ENVIRONMENT

A. There is little or no competition.

B. The competition is beginning to emerge because of the growth potential in the market.

C. There are many competitors, several of which are significant rivals.

D. There are just a few competitors who dominate the market.

4. CORPORATE FOCUS

A. We are focused on generating new sales above everything else; survival is a big concern.

B. We are focused on stabilizing operations so that we can accommodate and capitalize on growth opportunities.

C. We are focused on figuring out where new growth will come from, and how to reorganize to best position ourselves for the future.

D. We are focused on doing our best to squeeze out every last opportunity that is left in our market.

5. RISK TOLERANCE

A. Risks are taken every day by everyone in the company; it's the only way we will survive.

B. Risks are less attractive now—we have figured out what works and will continue to refine it.

C. We are at a point where we need to begin taking more risks than we used to in order to discover new growth opportunities.

D. The company is extremely risk-averse; we stick to what we have always known best and will not diverge from that.

6. AGILITY AND FLEXIBILITY

A. The company moves aggressively and quickly to seize new opportunities.

B. The company is somewhat agile and flexible, but we try to balance it out with an operational structure.

C. The company has lost some of its agility and flexibility because of operational demands.

D. The company is very slow to move and is locked into certain behaviors.

7. STRUCTURES AND SYSTEMS

A. There are very few structures or systems. That is not a priority.

B. We are spending a lot of time establishing structures and systems to become more efficient.

C. We have outgrown the existing structures and systems which used to work fine.

D. The structures and systems have not changed much over the years; they are so entrenched in the company that it will be difficult to make any changes.

8. WORK ENVIRONMENT

A. Our company is like a family. We are all very close and everyone tries to chip in to do whatever needs to get done.

B. The employees are close-knit and work well together, but we are also trying to "professionalize" the business environment by introducing policies, procedures, and job descriptions.

C. We operate as a professionally managed company, with clear roles, responsibilities, and lines of management authority.

D. The company is very bureaucratic, with lots of politics, power struggles, and turf wars.

9. CUSTOMER INTERACTION

A. We are intimate with customers, because we are desperate to find out what they need and then deliver whatever products or services they want.

B. We have good relationships with customers, and work hard to deliver consistently high levels of quality and service.

C. We operate mostly on assumptions about our customers that are based on our experience with them from the past.

D. We have lost touch with customers and are losing client accounts because their needs and preferences have changed.

10. COMMUNICATION

A. Communication is not an issue—everyone knows everything that is going on.

B. We are getting more organized about how to communicate internally and are for the first time developing clear channels of communication.

C. Our existing channels of communication are breaking down, both between departments and from leaders to employees.

D. Lines of communication have become more like walls that keep people in different departments and at different management levels apart from each other.

11. OPERATIONAL MANAGEMENT/PERFORMANCE

A. Operations are a low priority in the company compared to generating sales.

B. Operations are becoming a high priority. Each new operational improvement enhances the overall performance and productivity of the company.

C. Operational effectiveness is a key issue—we can't figure out why we're not getting more results from our efforts.

D. Operations are well established and would be difficult to change.

12. PROACTIVE/REACTIVE

A. The company is extremely aggressive and proactive, seizing every opportunity that comes along.

B. The company is proactive and aggressive, but focused.

C. The company is facing many new changes, both from the external market and internally, which force us into a reactive stance.

D. The company is operating from a totally reactive stance; we are even passive at times.

SCORING

Score your answers as follows:

A = 1

B = 2

C = 3

D = 4

If your total score was 12–20, your company is in Stage 1, start-up. You will continue to focus on being creative, flexible, and agile in order to get new sales until you establish a market niche that has strong growth potential.

If your score was 21–30, your company is in Stage 2, rapid growth.
You have established a market and will focus on operational infrastructure in order to accommodate volume and improve efficiencies.

If your score was 31–40, your company is in Stage 3, transition. The changes in your industry and the marketplace, along with limits to operational capacity, are forcing your company to reevaluate the existing strategies and business models and to find new avenues for growth and profitability. If you succeed at making these shifts you will begin a new growth cycle. If not, you will stagnate or decline.

If your score was 41–48, your company is declining. It is sticking to old strategies and structures while the world around you has changed. This will cause you to miss out on opportunities for new growth. Old formulas for success are entrenched in the organization, even though they are not working anymore. This makes it very difficult to make the changes that the competitive market is requiring of you. A great effort from the organization is necessary to make the shifts and changes required to enter a new growth cycle.

CHAPTER 2

Breaking Through: Managing the Transition to the Next Level

Growth is not easy. The transition from one level to the next is rarely smooth, owing to the complex dynamics that emerge during Stage 3. Turbulence, chaos, and confusion are necessary precedents to breaking through to new levels of performance. The stress of being caught between one growth curve and the next can cause the leadership team to behave in an unproductive manner. Management styles begin to crop up that actually hold the company back rather than propel it forward through the transition. The company's identity becomes challenged. People start complaining about "the good old days" and wonder if growth is really such a good idea after all.

These unpleasant conditions are indications that the patterns of behavior from earlier days are not working anymore, and that the company must change if it is to move forward.

IDENTITY CRISIS

When a growing company gets stuck in Stage 3, between the decline of one growth curve and the beginning of the next, it often experiences an identity crisis. The company doesn't want to lose the drive, spirit, and flexibility that made it successful; yet it also doesn't want to become bureaucratic, sluggish, and formal—the stereotypical negative qualities of large corporations. It is people in these companies that I often hear saying, "We're certainly not a big company, but we're not small anymore, either. We're not sure what we are!" Many of the characteristics of Stage 1 are attractive and appealing to business builders, and they fear that growth may destroy the very essence of what defines them as entrepreneurs.

Because of this ambivalence, some companies refuse to design employee policies, procedures, and organizational charts for fear that these will somehow corrupt their organizational agility and quickness. Getting organized does not erode competitive ability. In fact, few people can work effectively without structure and predictability. It is a company's *resistance to change* that will deflate corporate performance.

Many companies experience problems in high-growth environments because, although they achieve revenue growth, they simply aren't growing up organizationally. The firm may have annual sales of $15 million, but it behaves as if it were still a $3 million company. The owner is involved in every aspect of the business. No professional management is in place. Job descriptions don't exist. Information systems are inadequate. Performance standards are lacking. And crisis management is a way of life. As time goes on, these inefficiencies not only waste time and energy but also endanger profits. Ultimately, the company reaches the limit of its own capacities. Unless it transforms itself, it stops growing.

GETTING UNSTUCK BECAUSE OF A CRISIS

Some companies move forward only after a major crisis threatens their existence, forcing them into a "do or die" situation. Like people who change dramatically after a close call with death, companies transform themselves when faced with corporate demise. The crisis can have many sources. For instance, the customer who represents the majority of a company's sales may disappear, go out of business, or depart to a competitor. Or the bank may call in the firm's loan. Or the business's star employee—the one who has been critical to pulling operations together—gets fed up and leaves. Some companies in retrospect view these sobering experiences as acts of grace that force them to develop more effective systems, controls, or strategies, which allow them to rise to a new level of performance.

In his book *Entrepreneurs in High Technology* (Oxford University Press, 1991), Edward Roberts shows that many high-tech entrepreneurial companies experience a critical event that propels them from one level of growth to the next. This critical event, according to Roberts, is "a period in time during which a series of actions occur that bring about comprehensive changes in management structure, and the financial, marketing and planning processes" (page 333). Roberts contends that this transitional event is generally brought on indirectly by external situations, such as the board of directors firing the CEO, or an acquisition or sellout. At this critical juncture, the company makes the necessary changes to survive.

GROWTH BARRIERS

When a company is unable to break through from one level of growth to the next, it may be perpetuating its inertia with some unhealthy management styles that actually are Growth Barriers holding companies back from achieving their full growth potential. Growth Barriers are often internally generated, taking the form of unproductive behavior and attitudes from the business leader or executive management team. Inconsequential during the earlier stages of the company's growth, these behaviors and attitudes become a company's biggest barrier to new growth.

Five growth barriers that threaten companies during the Transition stage are (1) the Treadmill Mentality, (2) Management by Insanity, (3) Rearview-Mirror Management, (4) Management by ESP, and (5) Midas Touch Management. Let's look at each one in depth.

The Treadmill Mentality

People are working harder than ever, but the organization does not move forward. Among managers and employees the prevailing attitude is "We should be doing much better than this." But no consensus exists about what the company's problems are and what needs to be done to correct them. Everyone is so frantic that no one can step back to analyze the situation and plan for the future.

Treadmill Mentality companies are always in a panic, unable to catch their breath. Crisis management is a way of life. When a company is in Stage 3, increased efforts generally do not lead to better results. Although working harder can generate substantial progress during Stage 2, once a company enters the Transition Stage, it must break with old patterns of behavior in order to move to the next growth curve. New strategies, business practices, and patterns of behavior are necessary. But instead, Treadmill Mentality companies try to cope by pushing harder—working longer hours, knocking on more doors—and doing more of the same. Unfortunately, employees burn out when they don't see results or receive rewards for their efforts.

Paul Eldrenkamp, founder of Byggmeister Associates, a home remodeling company, knows exactly what the Treadmill Mentality feels like. After six years of being in business, revenues were up 25 percent, closing in on half a million dollars. Yet Byggmeister was barely breaking even. And Eldrenkamp paid himself only $27,149 even though he was working 60 hours a week. He knew something was wrong but he didn't know what. It certainly wasn't the quality of the work. His clients had taken to calling him Saint Paul because they liked what he did so much.

That is why Eldrenkamp found himself in a Howard Johnson's hotel at a meeting run by Business Networks, an organization of industry-specific groups that offer support, guidance, and constructive criticism to business owners. Paul's inquisitors were all remodelers but from other geographic markets. They had studied Eldrenkamp's books. They had visited his home office. They had talked to his clients, his subcontractors, and his employees. And they found much to criticize. His hiring practices. His financials. The way he charged his customers. His use of cash flow.

"What really hit me was how totally unsustainable our efforts had been," he says now. "Here was an endeavor that I was so close to, that I had spent so much of my adult life on. . . . We were going to go under if I didn't take some action."

The Treadmill Mentality characterizes a company that has never matured through Stage 2. For example, no matter how long Sean Durham, president of Leveraged Technology, a $21 million computer consulting firm in New York City, and Eric Rabinowitz, president of IHS, its subsidiary, spent poring over their weekly status reports they couldn't seem to pinpoint the source of one perplexing problem—why IHS HelpDesk Service's revenues were nearly 20 percent short of their projections. In the seven years since Rabinowitz had written the business plan for IHS, the company's market segment—supplying on-site contract workers to staff internal technical-support lines at *Fortune* 500 companies—had exploded, which enabled IHS to double its revenues every year. Until 1996, that is. "We thought we were concentrating on the right things to grow the business," says Rabinowitz, who notes that the two had aimed their efforts at marketing and recruiting. "But we were basically ruining the place."

Not that their efforts weren't plainly visible in August 1996. Thanks to an intensive direct-mail program, the company had no shortage of customers. Their strategy entailed frequent mailings to prospects and clients to keep IHS firmly implanted in their minds, by showering them with such offbeat premiums as miniature crystal balls, packets of forget-me-not seeds, and worry dolls. What mattered most was the continual reminders of the company's existence. The system was paying off: Every month IHS was receiving at least 60 requisitions—orders from a customer for an on-site analyst—a sixfold increase in eight months.

IHS kept up with that demand as best it could. If Rabinowitz couldn't recruit folks with the ideal technical background, he wasn't above drafting particularly friendly busboys and flight attendants. Well aware that it took certain personality traits to work on a help desk— empathy, intensity, endless patience—in 1994 he had begun using personality tests to screen candidates. Unsatisfied with the 12 tests he tried, Eric enlisted a consultant to develop a standardized test.

All of Durham and Rabinowitz's efforts were targeted toward boosting what they considered the company's critical number—the count of employees "on billing," or at a customer site generating revenues. In August 1996, IHS had 139 employees on billing; by December 1996 that figure had risen to 160. Still, Rabinowitz and Durham had projected sales of $13 million for IHS in fiscal 1997, but two months into that fiscal year, projected revenues were running closer to $11 million.

Rabinowitz and Durham couldn't deny that they had been missing opportunities to generate revenues: Of those 60 to 80 monthly requisitions, they were typically able to fill only about half. Why was that, exactly? As they cast their eyes over the employee trend analysis—a report that usually earned not more than a collective glance—the answers started to come into focus. The report, which listed the weekly count of employee arrivals and departures, showed a distinctly unhealthful trend. During the summer of 1996, rare was the week when newbies outnumbered quitters. And the weeks were adding up. According to the company's statistician, annual turnover for 1996 was likely to set a record: 300 percent. What's more, 30 percent of new hires weren't staying even as long as three months. "Our recruiters were working double time just to maintain the current level of business," says Durham.

Turnover looked like an increasingly insidious threat. Rising requisitions could absorb some of the costs, but for how long? What if new business fell off to the levels they had seen just six months earlier? "We thought, 'If the turnover continues and the reqs die off, we're in deep trouble,'" says Rabinowitz. "Maybe even out of business."

Despite the hard work and lack of progress, Treadmill Mentality companies create their own limitations to growth. They refuse to take the time to analyze the business and develop a plan to adapt new systems, structures, or patterns of behavior. They're too busy! If they take a moment to step off the treadmill, they fear that the whole business will fall apart. A lack of systems and structures is acceptable, and even desirable, when a company is in Stage 1. But not as it matures. The tyranny of the urgent is sometimes imagined, sometimes real. But despite all the efforts, if it is not addressed, a company will never break through to the next level of growth.

Management by Insanity

One definition of corporate insanity is "Doing things the same as they've always been done, but expecting different results." Management by Insanity companies enthusiastically identify new markets, strategies, or opportunities for growth and improvement, and spend a lot of time talking about them. But nothing changes. There is no follow-through, no analysis, and no clear plan. Employees become confused about the company's direction and strategy, because it seems to change week by week.

Beth, a manager at an East Coast nonprofit organization, is constantly frustrated by the behavior of the chief executive, George, who is always full of great ideas. He is a never-ending source of new strategies, markets, and services. Over the past few months, George called Beth into his office on a weekly basis and enthusiastically presented the Next Big Thing.

During the days that followed each weekly meeting, Beth frantically tried to implement George's ideas. But by the next weekly meeting, George was on to something else. There was never any follow-through in terms of research, strategy, planning, or committing resources—it was all hot air. Eventually Beth wised up. She stopped paying attention to George's creative outbursts. Her standard response became "That sounds great, George," but she tuned him out.

Like George, many entrepreneurs have big ideas. That's what helped make their business succeed in the beginning. But some never learn how to select the best ideas and follow through. Without such focus, a business and its employees are pulled in several directions, or in no direction at all. The organization becomes stuck in the swirl of the Transition cycle, unable to break into the next curve.

Rearview-Mirror Management

You can't drive a car by looking only in the rearview mirror. Rearview-Mirror Management means that a company knows where it's been, but doesn't look at where it's going. It is managing for what the company used to be, not for what it will become.

Business success is wonderful. But it can also become a trap if the organization clings too closely to the formulas that worked so well in the past. Past success is never a good predictor of future success, because the future is never simply an extension of the past. New variables are constantly introduced from the marketplace—from shifting customer demands and industry trends to innovations in technology, changing demographics, and globalization. All of these call on the business leader to pioneer new territory. But sometimes the patterns of previous success can be so ingrained in a company's instincts and reactions that it can't break out of them. When a company is only able to behave one way— the way that worked in the past—it is engaging in Rearview-Mirror Management.

A great example of this is IBM in the early 1990s. IBM was so heavily invested in selling mainframe computers, the market where it had been tremendously successful in the past, that it almost missed the personal computer market. IBM didn't initiate real change until Lou Gerstner, a man with no computer industry background, became CEO. Gerstner hadn't been driving in IBM's mainframe years, and his vision was not locked on the rearview mirror. Instead, he was looking out the front windshield.

This was not the case with the Children's Bookstore in Chicago, which closed its doors in 1997 after nearly a dozen years of operation. In

1985, owner Andy Laties and his wife combined his children's theater experience with her business background to create a retail store whose ambitious program of events would turn it into a community resource. At its peak, the store held about 250 events a year, including readings, dance recitals, author visits, and art workshops.

One key to the store's demise, Laties says, was the decision in 1992 not to expand but to remain focused on the nearby community. "If we had tried to grow very sharply in this market by bringing venture capital and doing an aggressive expansion, we'd still be in business," he remarks. "We could have gone to ten thousand-square-foot locations in the late 1980s, but we made the conscious decision not to. I was still doing two story hours a week and I didn't want to become an executive."

In 1995, walk-in sales dropped to $250,000, half the store's peak of $500,000 in 1991. Five superstores opened within a one-mile radius of the bookstore, nearly quadrupling the amount of retail space for children's books, 15,000 square feet, while population growth in the region was flat.

Laties says, "I'd have loved to continue running a children's bookstore with twenty-five thousand titles, an expert staff, lots of special events, and free story hours. I don't think there's any place in Chicago that can support that type of store anymore."

Rearview-Mirror Management companies normally have lots of awards, stacks of letters of congratulations, tons of pictures of the CEO with VIPs. These accolades hang in the lobby for every employee to see as they walk in each day. It's as if they are being told, "Relax! We are sooo successful . . . You have nothing to worry about." Unfortunately, they do.

There's nothing wrong with celebrating an achievement, or using awards and success stories for PR or to boost credibility with customers. But the truth is that basking in recent success is a dangerous place to be psychologically. Too many pats on the back or basking in past achievements can create a complacent attitude among employees. While one company is admiring the awards plastered on its lobby halls, its competitors are feeling a sense of urgency and desperation. This drives them to be a more creative and committed band of employees.

When it comes to growth strategies, Rearview-Mirror Management company executives always do the same thing: They pull out last year's budgets, ask salespeople how much more they think they can do next year, adjust for overhead, and *voilà!* They have next year's strategic plan. These companies give no attention to emerging marketplace trends. They ask no questions about how the company can best capitalize on new opportunities. They are unaware of what competitors are doing. The danger is that one day they will get a big surprise—a head-on collision with a competitor or shift in the market that appears to come out of the blue. If companies are looking out the driver's window instead of the rearview mirror, they can avoid a crash.

Management by ESP

One of the most important jobs of the CEO is to communicate effectively. Yet as they grow their business, few CEOs work at improving their communication skills. When asked about the company's direction, goals, and strategic plan, many CEOs respond by saying, "I don't have anything written down. It's in my head." They believe a "head" plan is equal to, or more reliable than, a written one. Even so, management and staff are expected to understand it, commit to it, and align their daily decisions with it. In most companies, such lack of clear communication leads to erratic decision-making, misunderstandings about performance, and inconsistent leadership from the CEO.

In the early stages of growth, relying on an entrepreneur's instincts and gut reactions is a reasonable approach to business. In fact, it is probably the best approach. If a strategic plan gets written too early, or is too detailed, it gets set aside once the business is up and running. However, in Stage 2, as the organization becomes more complex, with increasing numbers of employees, customers, and business systems, it requires more sophisticated methods of coordination and communication. A written plan pulls the employees' behavior and the company's activities in the direction intended by the CEO.

A written plan is exactly what H&H Bail Bonds needs as it tries to handle the results of explosive growth. Started in 1988 by CEO Ray Hrdlicka as a response to a tradition-bound industry, H&H enjoyed initial success in San Jose, California, by providing new levels of service and professionalism. Hrdlicka broke new ground by introducing credit checks, computers, and flexible organizational structure. By the late 1990s, H&H had expanded to seven other states and had 240 employees. It was hitting a wall. "My biggest problems are translating my vision of the company to employees, training them, and breaking down barriers between departments," says Hrdlicka.

To achieve breakthrough growth, a company must behave in new ways, develop new strategies, and establish new organizational patterns. This requires the CEO to communicate often, and in as many ways as possible. Without such effort, a company will experience breakdowns. The CEO may *think* that he has effectively communicated a goal or strategy, but if he communicated with different people in different departments at different times, each employee puts his or her own spin on the information. The result: The performance of individuals and the company is inconsistent and erratic. Decisions are made, then changed, then overridden. Leadership becomes questioned.

Kirk Hankins, CEO of $12 million Winland Electronics in Minneapolis admits he managed by ESP for years without realizing it. "People became frustrated over what were probably the little things," he says.

For instance, Winland Electronics had historically spent extensive time on new product development—something both the engineers and the marketing department enjoyed. The company was constantly brimming with new ideas. But because Winland Electronics had limited engineering talent, Hankins decided it should not develop any more new products unless a customer funded the enterprise. To Hankins, his logic was clear: Don't get involved with projects unless you're getting paid for them. In addition, Hankins thought it was sound business strategy to lock customers in at the product development stage. It was a simple strategy to Hankins, but not to the engineers and marketing people who had been working under a different scenario for years. Unfortunately, Hankins never communicated his rationale with anyone. Instead, he just stopped product development. Hankins just took it for granted that he made a good decision, and never thought much about how that decision impacted others in the company.

When the engineers and the marketing department tried to introduce new product ideas, Hankins said no. They didn't understand what he was thinking and why their ideas weren't being considered anymore. Although he wasn't facing a mutiny, his lack of communication did impact morale. Eventually, Hankins realized that he needed to explain the strategy straight out to the entire company in order to get people behind it.

His strategy turned out to be a winner. Winland Electronics now has teams from engineering and the marketing department working closely with customers to design and manufacture products that fit customized specifications. And the company grew almost twofold in the year that followed.

Another company, a technology consulting and training firm in the Northeast, had a smart, hard-working, and committed group of managers. But when asked whether they understood the company's goals and strategies, they replied, "We are committed to this company. We just wish we knew where it was headed!" The company had plateaued, with sales declining for the past two years. To upgrade their leadership role and status in the company, the owners had formed themselves into a board of directors. They would meet behind closed doors on a monthly basis. In spite of several months of such high-level discussions, *they never informed managers what they said regarding the company's future strategies.* Because of the ambiguity and lack of communication, employee commitment eroded and many employees left. The turnover put the company even further behind in jumping the curve.

Midas Touch Management

Arrogance is a dangerous business attitude. When a company becomes too enamored with its own technology, products, or services, it can easily lose touch with the outside world. By the time it notices new industry trends, or shifts in competition and customer needs, the window of opportunity has been lost. This lack of corporate humility causes a company to become internally focused, oblivious to both threats and opportunities in the marketplace. Management may spend enormous amounts of time and money to develop a superior new product, but it never asks, "What do our customers think?" Instead it believes, "If we create it, the world will beat a path to our door." It thinks it has the Midas touch. Unfortunately, this is rarely the case.

That's what happened to Main Street Muffins. "If your business gets off to a great start, it's easy to think you have the Midas touch," says founder Steven Marks. "Why not try this, that, and the other thing?" When Marks and his partner, Harvey Nelson, started Main Street Muffins, in 1987, they felt they could do no wrong. They raised $75,000 from investors and another $100,000 in government-subsidized loans and grants. They renovated a condemned building in downtown Akron, and 3,000 people came through their doors on the first day the retail bakery was open. "At twenty-seven I felt euphoric about my lifelong dream's coming true. Local newspapers were clamoring to tell our story, and we were only too happy to tell it. It was exhilarating." Until the company nearly went bankrupt.

During its first year Main Street Muffins attracted a loyal following, and it became a popular breakfast and lunch spot. Then, in 1988, out of the blue, the company received a call from a local restaurateur. He wondered if they could sell him their muffin batter so he could bake muffins in his restaurant rather than buy muffins from the store. "We jumped into the frozen-muffin-batter business with both feet, having no idea where it might lead," says Marks. They purchased buckets and additional equipment, developed systems, and began acquiring more business. "We felt we could do no wrong. It was such an exciting time. I couldn't wait to get up and go to work in the morning. We were fulfilling the American dream!"

The partners' confidence was so high that they thought they could tackle any project and succeed. So they decided to open another store. The bank lent $100,000 to buy a frozen-yogurt store that they would convert to a bakery—"further confirming our naïve belief in how savvy and ingenious we were," notes Marks. Over the next several months the "defrost, scoop out, and bake" frozen-muffin-batter business began to take off and was bringing in about 30 percent of total revenues.

But inside the business, things were not looking so rosy. It was a difficult time; the exciting opportunities were turning into problems. And those problems were stretching resources. Employee morale was low. Bakers were calling in sick at 3 A.M. One just up and quit one afternoon without any notice. The owners' heads were spinning. "We lost four employees out of a total of sixteen during nine months from hell," recalls Marks. "Cash flow was so bad we were using four Visa cards to get from one period to the next. Production mistakes increased. Freezers broke down." In the midst of the turmoil, the company was paying less attention to its customers and ignoring their complaints. Gross margins slipped from more than 50 percent to less than 40 percent.

The strain was both mentally and physically draining for the partners. By mid-1989, both the retail stores and the batter business began a nosedive toward bankruptcy.

After a lot of wrenching discussions about whether they should let go of the business they had worked so hard to build, Marks and Nelson decided to sell their unprofitable retail stores, but with licensing agreements. The company would act as a licenser to the buyers, providing quality checks and the use of the name Main Street Muffins, and requiring that the licensees purchase the company's muffin, cookie, and brownie batters. That would provide the company with a sales base yet eliminate the day-to-day problems of running the retail outlets. In 1990 and 1991, they sold both stores, but at significant losses. In fact, they gave away the original store.

That painful yet necessary purging enabled the two partners and remaining employees to devote their attention to the frozen-batter business, under a new name: Main Street Gourmet. "Even though we knew we had a rough road ahead of us, we all felt tremendously relieved." Marks says. The excitement that accompanies a new business returned, and the quest to fulfill the American dream is back on track, with projected 1998 sales of $10 million.

ANALYSIS: YOUR COMPANY'S MANAGEMENT STYLE

Is your company experiencing one of the management styles that is a Growth Barrier? If so, you may be holding back growth.

Take this quiz to determine whether one of these management styles characterizes your company. Rate the following questions on a scale of 1 (to a small degree) to 5 (to a very large degree). Total the scores at the end of each category.

TREADMILL MENTALITY

1. People talk a lot about burnout.   1___ 2___ 3___ 4___ 5___
2. Crisis management is the norm.   1___ 2___ 3___ 4___ 5___
3. The company talks about planning but doesn't commit time to doing it.   1___ 2___ 3___ 4___ 5___
4. The pressure for performance is high, sometimes unbearable.
   1___ 2___ 3___ 4___ 5___
5. The management team never has time for professional development or vacations.   1___ 2___ 3___ 4___ 5___

TOTAL:____

MANAGEMENT BY INSANITY

1. Employees talk a lot about new ideas.
   1___ 2___ 3___ 4___ 5___

2. There is no sense of strategic priorities.
   1___ 2___ 3___ 4___ 5___

3. Many new strategies are explored but only at a surface level.
   1___ 2___ 3___ 4___ 5___

4. The company spent time planning, but there hasn't been any follow-through.   1___ 2___ 3___ 4___ 5___

5. Managers and departments follow their own agendas.
   1___ 2___ 3___ 4___ 5___

TOTAL:____

REARVIEW-MIRROR MANAGEMENT

1. Employees talk about past performance more than the future.
   1___ 2___ 3___ 4___ 5___

2. Strategic priorities never change. They have been locked in for years.   1___ 2___ 3___ 4___ 5___

3. Strategies are based on historical budgeting—just manipulating the numbers.   1___ 2___ 3___ 4___ 5___

4. There is no need for planning, just budgeting.

   1___ 2___ 3___ 4___ 5___

5. Managers are generally satisfied with their performance and are complacent.   1___ 2___ 3___ 4___ 5___

TOTAL:____

MANAGEMENT BY ESP

1. People talk a lot about the last thing they heard the CEO mention.   1___ 2___ 3___ 4___ 5___

2. Strategic priorities are either vague, or constantly shifting.

   1___ 2___ 3___ 4___ 5___

3. New strategies are based on following the actions of the CEO.

   1___ 2___ 3___ 4___ 5___

4. There is never any planning—just conversations while passing in the halls.   1___ 2___ 3___ 4___ 5___

5. Managers are always second-guessing their performance.

1___ 2___ 3___ 4___ 5___

TOTAL:____

MIDAS TOUCH MANAGEMENT

1. People talk a lot about the company's cool product or service.

1___ 2___ 3___ 4___ 5___

2. Strategic priorities are tied to product development.

1___ 2___ 3___ 4___ 5___

3. New strategies are driven by technical or creative people.

1___ 2___ 3___ 4___ 5___

4. Planning is based solely on internal information.

1___ 2___ 3___ 4___ 5___

5. No one ever questions his or her performance.

1___ 2___ 3___ 4___ 5___

TOTAL:____

SCORING:

1–8: *Good, this is not your company.*

9–15: *Borderline. Your company may be slipping into or coming out of this management style.*

16–25: *You're in deep. Don't get stuck with this management style.*

Do you recognize your company from this test? These management styles represent normal issues companies confront prior to breaking through to the next level of growth. Managers need to pay attention to these dysfunctional trends as they emerge in their companies, because they are signs of change. They are indications that patterns of behavior from earlier days are not working anymore, and the company must change in order to make progress. These behaviors only become truly problematic when they don't get resolved—when leaders fail to initiate change, and allow the growth barriers to perpetuate over time. If this happens, the company will either become stuck at that level, or it will disintegrate.

GROWTH DRIVERS: KEYS TO NAVIGATING THE TRANSITIONS OF GROWTH

Many companies have grappled with the challenges of growth and have emerged successfully on the other side. But what did it take to get through? What clues have these companies left behind about their success? And how can those lessons be applied in your own company?

I have identified several management practices that contribute to breaking through to the next level. These *Growth Drivers* not only are characteristics of successful growth companies but also are business disciplines that get hard-wired into the company's culture. Growth Drivers are the *tools* to help companies navigate their way through the growth cycle.

The following chapters discuss each Growth Driver in depth, and provide exercises and tools for executing them in your own company. But first, a brief description of each.

Market Intelligence

Market Intelligence is a company's ability to recognize and adapt to changes in the external marketplace. The external marketplace comprises customers, competitors, the industry as a whole, and emerging trends (both within and outside the industry) that shape the future. This external environment is constantly shifting and evolving. To recognize and act on these marketplace shifts, a company must effectively gather information from the world around it. This information must be used as a strategic tool to leverage new opportunities. Without market intelligence, a company lags behind in competing for and meeting customers' expectations, and will ultimately miss out on opportunities for growth.

Strategic Leadership

Strategic Leadership refers to a clear source of delegation, decision-making and long-term planning within an organization, and the *personal responsibility* that is required to effect this caliber of leadership. Usually the CEO provides strategic leadership, although this responsibility sometimes resides among several partners, owners, or a leadership team.

The characteristics of effective leadership change as a company grows. The leadership skills that bring a company to one level of growth may not necessarily be the same type or level of skills that brings a company to the next. As one successful CEO of a growing plumbing-heating contracting business told me, "The technical aspect of what my company does is becoming less and less important. In fact, I am personally not in the plumbing business anymore. I'm in the business of managing a growing company."

It is up to the individual leader of a company to develop his or her leadership skills according to what the company needs.

Clarity of Purpose

Clarity of Purpose builds a strong, loyal group of employees with high levels of commitment to achieving corporate goals. Most successful growth companies are focused: They know what business they are in and, more important, what business they are not in. And they have very clear, ambitious goals for the company's future. These companies have a strong identity and direction and understand their own uniqueness and the ways they add value for their customers. They also have bold aspirations for the future and they aspire to reach clearly defined landmarks. Most important, a company's identity and focus are more than just a mission statement contrived by the CEO and displayed on a plaque in the lobby. They are deeply embedded in the corporate culture and are shared by all employees.

Strategic Planning

Strategic Planning is the process by which an organization turns its dreams into reality. It results in a roadmap for achieving the company's purpose and direction, outlining the specifics of what needs to be done, when, how and by whom. It turns a company's future aspirations into specific tasks on a specific schedule.

As a company grows and becomes more complex, planning becomes a key management discipline. It ensures that the proper activities are taking place at the right time to move the organization consistently toward its goals. Without planning, the company runs the risk of operating in a reactive stance—responding to the environment rather than designing the future. As the number of employees, managers, customers, competitors, the marketplace threats, and opportunities increase, the decision-making process becomes more complicated. Planning facilitates the development of priorities that are clearly understood by management and staff.

Internal Infrastructure

In the physical world, infrastructure refers to the roads, runways, bridges, drainage, etc., that support the flow of traffic. Without these, what happens? Traffic jams up; people can't move easily. Corporate Internal Infrastructure refers to the procedures and systems that support the execution of the company's strategic plan and the organization's growth. The Internal Infrastructure includes the company's organizational structure (who does what), business systems (how things get done), and financial controls (how performance is monitored). As a company grows, it must continually monitor its Internal Infrastructure to accommodate growth. A colleague of mine puts it this way: A company without a solid infrastructure feels as if it is propped up with toothpicks.

THE GROWTH STRATEGY ANALYSIS

How well is your company prepared to manage growth? Is your company building a solid platform for growth? Or is it stumbling over the many obstacles that hobble companies during the growth process? The Growth Strategy Analysis exercise that follows is designed to help you answer those questions. Using the criteria of the five Growth Drivers, it provides an interactive method to view objectively your company's strengths and weaknesses in the context of long-term growth.

Each Growth Driver is analyzed using five questions to which you must respond with a rating on a scale of 0 to 3. Total your scores for each category. By the end, you will have five totals, one for each Growth Driver, showing how your company measures up in that area. The highest level, "one step ahead," indicates that your company is well prepared for growth in that critical business area. The second level, "getting by," means you can get by with your current level of performance in that area, but eventually you'll be vulnerable if this area is not addressed and improved. The third level, "behind the pack," means that this area will impede your company's growth and is likely causing current business problems.

Getting Input from Others

You may find that others in your company do not have the same point of view as you. Get input and opinions from others on your management team by giving them copies of the survey and having them respond individually. Then get together and compare notes. That exercise will be sure to generate some interesting discussion about your company's strengths, weaknesses, and priorities for action.

THE GROWTH STRATEGY ANALYSIS

0 = Not at all
1 = To a small degree
2 = To a moderate degree
3 = To a high degree

MARKET INTELLIGENCE

Market Intelligence refers to a company's ability to perceive and adapt to changes in the marketplace.

1. Are you crystal-clear on who your customers are and why they use your products/services?   0___ 1___ 2___ 3 _3_

2. Is there a person or group of people in the company responsible and accountable for marketing, market research, and keeping up with industry trends (through research, trade shows, industry journals, etc.)?   0___ 1___ 2___ 3 _3_

3. Do you know the strengths, weaknesses, strategies, and financial status of your top five competitors?   0___ 1___ 2 _2_ 3___

4. Do you have mechanisms in place to gather customer feedback on an ongoing basis?   0___ 1___ 2 _2_ 3___

5. Have you made changes, innovations, or modifications from the original product/service concept?   0___ 1___ 2___ 3 _3_

TOTAL: _13_

STRATEGIC LEADERSHIP

Strategic Leadership is a CEO's ability to provide clear direction, decision-making, and long-term planning.

1. Does the CEO spend a consistent, dedicated amount of time on strategic thinking and long-term planning, rather than being trapped in day-to-day operations?   0___ 1___ 2 _2_ 3___

2. Is the CEO open to challenging the status quo?
   0___ 1___ 2___ 3 _3_

3. Does the CEO delegate appropriately, rather than making every decision?   0___ 1 _1_ 2___ 3___

4. Does the CEO effectively communicate the corporate direction, strategies, and goals to employees?
   0___ 1___ 2 _2_ 3___

5. Is the leadership team united and focused on achieving the same goals and direction for the business?
   0___ 1 _1_ 2___ 3___

TOTAL: _9_

CLARITY OF PURPOSE

Clarity of Purpose is a shared understanding of the company's identity and a detailed picture of the company's direction in the future.

1. Have you articulated in writing why your company is uniquely different from any other company in the world, and what the company's ideal future looks like?   0___ 1___ 2 _2_ 3___

2. Is the company operating from a platform of its unique strengths, skills and talents, rather than being "all things to all people"?   0___ 1___ 2___ 3 _3_

3. Is the future vision of the company shared by all members of the management team?   0___ 1___ 2___ 3 _3_

4. Is the purpose and direction of the company communicated to all employees?   0___ 1___ 2 _2_ 3___

5. Do employees commit and contribute to the basic purpose and future direction of the company on a day-to-day basis?
   0___ 1 _1_ 2___ 3___

TOTAL: _11_

STRATEGIC PLANNING

Strategic Planning is the process by which the company determines specific action steps to achieve future goals.

1. Does the company have a regular planning process for reviewing and updating its strategies and execution?
0___ 1✗ 2___ 3___

2. Has the company set clearly defined, achievable goals for a one-year, three-year, and five-year time frame?
0___ 1✗ 2___ 3___

3. Is strategy development based on qualitative variables in the marketplace rather than on historical budgeting?
0___ 1___ 2___ 3_3_

4. Do managers work together in developing corporate strategy, as opposed to setting independent goals and agendas for their individual departments? 0___ 1___ 2___ 3_3_

5. Does the strategy translate into specific, timely, and measurable tactics? 0___ 1___ 2_2_ 3___

TOTAL:____

INTERNAL INFRASTRUCTURE

Internal Infrastructure is the company's ability to support its business strategies through its internal operations, systems, and organizational structures.

1. Are the roles and responsibilities for each employee clearly defined? 0___ 1___ 2___ 3_✗_

2. Are the financial systems in place to get accurate and timely data on both current and projected financial performance?
0___ 1___ 2___ 3_✗_

3. Is employee compensation aligned with corporate goals and strategies? 0___ 1___ 2___ 3_✗_

4. Is technology being utilized effectively to improve overall performance? 0___ 1___ 2___ 3_✗_

5. Are effective policies and procedures in place to help employees do their jobs and make it easy for customers to do business with your company? 0___ 1___ 2_✗_ 3___

TOTAL:_16_

SCORING

0–5: *Level 1—Behind the pack*
6–10: *Level 2—Getting by*
11–15: *Level 3—One step ahead*

How did your company score? In the box following, place an X in the appropriate cell for each category, according to your score. This gives you an at-a-glance indication of where you need to focus to grow effectively.

GROWTH STRATEGY MATRIX

GROWTH DRIVER	LEVEL ONE	LEVEL TWO	LEVEL THREE
Market Intelligence			✕
Strategic Leadership		✕	
Clarity of Purpose			✕
Strategic Planning		✕	
Internal Infrastructure			✕

THE GROWTH STATEGY ANALYSIS

Scoring Market Intelligence

Level 1: Behind the pack. Your company is not paying attention to the external environment and is focusing its activities, efforts, resources, and priorities internally. This is a dangerous and vulnerable position, as changes in industry trends, competition, or customer demands may catch you off guard, without giving you enough time to catch up.

Level 2: Getting by. Your company recognizes the importance of Market Intelligence, and is making efforts to stay in touch with the marketplace. However, one of your competitors may be doing a better job of it and getting a stranglehold on an opportunity or niche that could have been yours.

Level 3: One step ahead. Your company is poised to take a leadership position in the marketplace by proactively identifying opportunities early enough to make high-leverage strategic decisions and take appropriate action.

Scoring Strategic Leadership

Level 1: Behind the pack. Your company lacks the leadership necessary to take it to the next level of growth. As long as the CEO is thinking and acting as though he or she is running a mom-and-pop shop, that is exactly what the company will be. The CEO must be removed from day-to-day operations to focus on the future growth of the business. In most companies at this level, the employees are starving for more leadership initiative from the CEO.

Level 2: Getting by. Your company has established the foundation for strategic leadership, but must ensure that the CEO's energy doesn't get sucked back into a short-term perspective. The CEO must communicate consistently with management and staff about his or her goals for the company. In addition, he or she must build consensus and commitment, and delegate accordingly.

Level 3: One step ahead. Your company has the right stuff for driving growth, and it has the foresight to position itself to be in the right place at the right time to take advantage of new opportunities. Stay on track by asking for feedback from employees to identify how to further improve the company, and the CEO's leadership skills.

Scoring Clarity of Purpose

Level 1: Behind the pack. Your company will have difficulty getting commitment and contributions from employees to work toward any one particular goal or strategy. Remember: The organization is not an independent entity; it's made up of individual people. If they don't all have a sense of purpose and direction for the work they are doing, then neither will the company.

Level 2: Getting by. Your company has most likely discussed or developed its core purpose and direction, but can develop them even further and use them as a tool to build enthusiasm and commitment from the staff. Try the group exercises in Chapter 5 with the management team to draw out more details of the future, and discuss the unique benefits your company brings to its customers. Then make sure the core purpose and direction are communicated throughout the organization as often and in as many ways as possible.

Level 3: One step ahead. Your company has a strong grip on its identity and where it is going. This will translate into the way the organization conducts business on a daily basis, and will build a strong leadership reputation in the business community. As a result, you will be more likely to attract and retain the best and brightest people who fit the corporate culture and who are willing to work hard for the company's future success.

Scoring Strategic Planning

Level 1: Behind the pack. As they say, if you don't know where you are going, any road will take you there. Your company utilizes little or no Strategic Planning, and is probably running by the seat of its pants. Although this loose management style is acceptable among start-up and small businesses in the early stages of growth, it is a serious red flag among more established companies. With a greater number of employees and customers, communicating, operating, and coordinating become much more complex, requiring a formal process for setting and achieving corporate goals.

Level 2: Getting by. Your company recognizes the importance of Strategic Planning, and can probably benefit from improvements on the planning process. Some ideas: Include the management team in the planning process; build strategies around core competencies, such as your innovative technology or your topnotch customer service; ensure a follow-up and feedback loop in execution; and avoid plans based on historical budgets.

Level 3: One step ahead. Your company has a sophisticated Strategic Planning process in place that will allow you to set and achieve substantial growth goals, with a clear roadmap for execution. If you haven't done so, consider using an outside facilitator to bring additional insights, ideas, and innovations into the process and potential outcomes.

Scoring Infrastructure

Level 1: Behind the pack. Your company is not prepared to accommodate additional growth with its current Infrastructure. It is important that your systems and structures accommodate current sales before you plan an aggressive growth strategy. Consider how to structure the organization around jobs that need to be done rather than the people you happen to have. Conduct a work-flow analysis to determine where the weakest links are, and address them immediately.

Level 2: Getting by. Your company is on track to handle growth, but needs to pay equal attention to operations as well as strategy. Do not avoid technology and the role it can play in easing operations and providing competitive advantage. Set up task forces with employees in high-priority functional areas to evaluate operations and determine opportunities for improvement.

Level 3: One step ahead. Your company has the important systems in place for growth, but beware of changes that will come with growth. The systems that work well for you now will inevitably become obsolete as the company grows and changes.

CHAPTER 3

Market Intelligence

M ARKET INTELLIGENCE, A COMPANY'S ABILITY TO UNDER-
stand and adapt to marketplace changes, is a key Growth Driver.
Firms that pay close attention to customers, market trends, the competitive environment, and industry-specific trends will be in the best position
to take advantage of new opportunities to achieve long-term growth.

An organization's capacity for gathering Market Intelligence
depends on whether the company is internally or externally focused.
Thriving growth companies are externally focused: They *systematically*
gather and analyze relevant information from the world around them
and then make strategic decisions on the basis of the data. In contrast,
internally focused companies discover critical information too late
because they spend insufficient time on this task. They soon fall back in
the competitive race because they are not responding to the dynamics of
business. Customers' choices, needs, and preferences constantly evolve.
Competitors shift strategies and tactics. New technology alters how
business is conducted. Waves of mergers and consolidations change the
competitive environment. A myriad of other factors can dramatically
challenge the way you compete today. When a company is insular, it
responds slowly to these changing realities.

The link between Market Intelligence and business growth in
entrepreneurial companies has been confirmed by leading business
researchers. A study published in *Business Horizons* (Jan./Feb., 1994)
compared two groups of entrepreneurial companies which had sales volumes of between $25 million and $150 million. All companies had

broken out of Stage 1 and had enjoyed substantial growth through Stage 2. However, one group had grown steadily year after year, while the other group had grown to a certain level and then had stopped. What happened? The stalled companies reached Stage 2 and got stuck there; the growth companies had successfully managed the Stage 3 transition and had made it to the next growth curve.

Researchers discovered that stalled companies "failed to understand and respond to the complex set of changing opportunities and obstacles that were developing outside the firm," whereas growth companies "focused on the external growth opportunities and obstacles, and had developed the internal competencies necessary to cope with environmental change."

The following management traits were key differences.

STALLED VERSUS GROWING COMPANIES

STALLED GROWTH	GROWING COMPANIES
Sales/product-driven approach to growth	Marketing-driven approach to growth
Internally focused	Externally focused
Modest investments in market research	Systematic market research
No one devoted to marketing or strategic management	Has marketing department or equivalent
Only modest changes in original market concept	Many changes in original market concept

(Source: *Business Horizons,* Jan./Feb., 1994. Used with permission.)

According to the study, successful companies saw the marketplace as their source of growth strategies. Consequently, they invested the time and resources to get appropriate feedback from the marketplace. They used that information to make strategic decisions that often involved changing how they did business.

In contrast, stalled companies were unaware of the external marketplace. They developed business strategies from an internal perspective, and maintained their existing business practices. When profits fell, they usually blamed salespeople and increased pressure on them to sell.

A firm that participated in the research project sheds some light on this misguided management tactic. Over an eight-year period, a manufacturers' representative of industrial electronic components had become a dominant player in the midwestern marketplace, with $20 million in annual sales. Success was attributed largely to the efforts of 30 highly trained technical salespeople. But then sales plateaued. In response, the company owner put increased pressure on the sales force, providing intensive sales training, and raising the quota for average weekly sales calls by 25 percent. Yet sales remained in a holding pattern. The owner continued to view the problem as sales ineffectiveness.

By being internally focused, the owner missed the significant changes his competitors were making in their marketing practices, and developments among the manufacturers the firm represented. Specifically, his competitors had switched selling tactics—one launched a major telemarketing effort, and another one set up a directly competitive sales force. In addition, one of the manufacturers represented by the company failed to develop a new product on time, providing a window of opportunity for other competitors.

All these changes in the marketplace helped stall the firm's growth. The company owner's focus on sales-driven solutions caused the firm to lose momentum and the sales force became demoralized.

In *Entrepreneurs in High Technology* (Oxford University Press, 1991), Edward B. Roberts studied 21 technology firms at various levels of success in an attempt to identify the contributing factors to their growth. Each firm had at least $5 million in sales revenue and had been in business for at least five years. Roberts found that the most successful firms had undergone a transformation from a technological-oriented to a more marketing-oriented strategic perspective. Firms that did not alter their strategic focus in the same way fell significantly behind the other companies' growth and financial performance. Some key changes these companies underwent include those shown in the table that follows.

TRANSFORMATION FROM TECHNOLOGY FOCUS
TO MARKETING FOCUS

FACTORS	BEFORE CHANGE	AFTER CHANGE
Market planning	Nonexistent	Formalized and integrated into strategic planning
Market research	None	In-house department
Control of new product development	CEO/engineering	Marketing or marketing and engineering
R&D concentration	Redesign, new product development	New product development
Management team	Founders	Managers hired from outside

Again, a company's marketing focus and Market Intelligence were significantly linked to growth. The externally focused companies invested in a marketing department and market research, and integrated market planning into Strategic Planning. Even new product development, once the domain of the technical experts, was handed over to the marketing department.

Inc.'s interviews with *Inc.* 500 companies also demonstrates the impact of Market Intelligence on growth. These successful growth companies had the ability to adjust to changing markets. If one product or market had become mature or too competitive, they would shift resources to another, related market or a submarket in which they could compete more effectively. These *Inc.* 500 companies were growing because of the entrepreneur's instinct that the company's activities needed to be market-driven.

MARKET INTELLIGENCE AND BUSINESS GROWTH

As the research cited attests, Market Intelligence is one of the most critical driving forces to push a company from one level of growth to the next. Those companies that are unable to focus their time and attention on the external marketplace will get stuck at the tail end of the first growth curve and stagnate or decline.

Why does a lack of Market Intelligence become an issue as companies grow? Once these companies have an established customer base and have reached a level of success, they start to operate on *assumptions* about their customers and the marketplace rather than on *data*. The customer intimacy that carried the company through its early stages of growth is lost. Operations (Stage 2) becomes the company's focal point, and in the process, customers are often forgotten. Before long, the market has moved in a new direction and customer wants and needs have changed. Yet the company still operates on assumptions that held true years ago. Future business strategies cannot be built on assumptions from the past.

"When you get too wrapped up in the office world, you lose touch with the customer, with the employee," says Elliot Goodwin, president of Larry's Shoes in Fort Worth, Texas. From 1986 to 1987 the company's sales soared from $14.5 million to $18.6 million. But then they began to dip in 1988, dropping to $18.2 million. It was in 1989, though—as a grand five-year plan was being drafted—that things began to unravel. The gain in that year's overall sales, to $22.2 million, came from a Houston store; the other stores' sales had plateaued—"sucking money out," is how Goodwin puts it—and Larry's came close to taking a loss. Goodwin was forced to look outward to get a glimpse of market forces that demanded responses.

In retrospect, Goodwin blames himself for the sales slowdown. "I was living in a corporate glass tower," he says. "I got immersed in the wholesale side, dealing with vendors who were showing me their hottest new products. Pretty soon you're dictating what the stores should be—I was analyzing from here what I thought the customers wanted and catapulting those ideas out to the units. That created a store-versus-corporate kind of environment, and morale began to deteriorate."

IS YOUR COMPANY INTERNALLY OR EXTERNALLY FOCUSED?

How can you tell if your company is too internally focused? Corporate priorities are a key indicator, priorities that are revealed in the behaviors and attitudes of management in the course of everyday business. The result is that the internally focused companies simply are not *doing* a lot of the things that externally focused companies are doing. Here is a checklist to test your company's focus. Answer true or false to the following questions:

1. We are generally too busy to spend time with our customers.
   True___ False_✕_

2. People in our company rarely get involved with professional development.   True_✕_ False___

3. The CEO is isolated from other CEOs in our community and industry.   True_✕_ False_＼_

4. Corporate strategies are driven from internal sources—technical, product development, operations, sales, or historical budgets.   True___ False_✕_

5. Customers are viewed as interruptions of our work.
   True___ False_✕_

6. We do not have any mechanisms to gather customer feedback from employees that have the most customer contact.
   True___ False_✕_

7. We haven't done market research in years.   True___ False_✕_

8. We can not define who our customers are.   True___ False_✕_

9. We do not have a marketing department or person in charge of marketing.   True___ False_✕_

10. We feel that we know better than the customers what they want.   True___ False_✕_

11. When the going gets tough, we get tough on the sales people.
    True___ False_✕_

If you answered true to more than four of those questions, your company is internally focused. It will run into a wall on its way up the growth curve. Getting stuck in the third stage of the growth curve is not advisable. Fortunately, practical tools exist that can be used to build Market Intelligence in your company.

FIVE STEPS TO BUILDING MARKET INTELLIGENCE

If you want your company to grow, you must make a determined choice to be externally focused. Market Intelligence provides a company with a steady stream of relevant data that will guide the firm's future growth strategies. But how do you build this competency? Where do you find the Market Intelligence that is relevant to your particular company? How do you capture that information? It is not difficult to answer these questions, nor is it expensive. But it does require commitment and diligence on your part.

Here are five steps to creating Market Intelligence. Each is a component of a practical approach to becoming externally focused.

Step 1. Embrace a Market-Driven Approach to Growth

As you assess your business situation and consider strategies for growth, approach the problem from the market's point of view. Don't ask, What do we think? Instead, ask, What do our customers think? What do our competitors think? What is happening in the marketplace right now that will impact how we do business? These fundamental questions drive growth strategies. Unfortunately, many management teams lay out their future plans for growth without getting *any* feedback from customers or the marketplace. Their excuse is that there is no time to consult the market, and there's no budget to do market research. But companies that get to the next level know that *strategies for growth cannot be considered without consulting the outside marketplace.*

"We have made a conscious, intentional decision to move from a product-driven company to a market-driven company," says Thom Schulz, owner of Group Publishing in Loveland, Colorado. With annual sales of $25 million, Group Publishing is an innovator in the field of Sunday School curriculum, providing churches with exciting and relevant materials for children and teens that was previously nonexistent in the Christian educational publishing industry. But along with Group Publishing's initial wave of success came knockoff imitations from the competition. And the competitors were not fly-by-night operations— they were large, well-established publishers with plenty of resources and marketing savvy. Group faced the harsh truth that even though its products were terrific, it couldn't compete effectively with those larger players unless it shifted its corporate mind-set to pay much closer attention to the marketplace.

"We've always felt that being an innovator was very important to our sense of identity, even if others were stealing and copying our product concepts." Schulz says. "But then we realized that this is not flattery, it's dangerous—we had a real threat on our hands." Schulz admits that it's not easy changing the mind set of his 180 employees to think in terms of the market rather than of the next great idea for a product, and it hasn't been an overnight transformation. But they are making significant strides, and the mood is upbeat. "Our meetings, language, and the core of our discussions here are now market-driven rather than product-driven. I spend a lot of time communicating this message, and everyone understands that is where we want to go."

Step 2. Invest in the Marketing Function Within the Organization

Growth companies invest in Market Intelligence by creating the appropriate positions for marketing within the organizational structure. Although not every growing company can afford a top-level marketing executive or a full-fledged marketing department, it is important to assign competent people to be responsible and accountable to carry out the marketing function. These individuals gather market data and interpret that information so as to align strategic company decisions with marketplace realities.

Ideally, an executive is responsible for market research and collaborates with the management team on making strategic decisions. Having a senior-level marketing executive ensures that this information is not neglected or delegated to managers who won't utilize it properly. Companies without such clearly defined positions for marketing will find that crucial market data fall by the wayside, because there is no one responsible. As a result, strategic decisions are based on little or no external information and businesses have difficulty growing.

Hiring a marketing executive was one of the most important decisions Group Publishing made toward achieving their goal of becoming a market-driven company. They had a fairly strong knowledge of the market and their customers, but certainly not at the level of sophistication that they would need to compete as a serious player in their industry. "We compare our company's growth to a football team," Thom Schulz says. "It's like taking a college football team to the NFL. Some players have the skills, some don't. We have to bring on new coaches and new talent to compete at that next level."

A big part of that management upgrade involved hiring a senior-level marketing executive, a player from the big league. The first step for Schultz and his team at Group was to realize what this meant in terms of pay scales. "We decided that if we wanted to step up to the professional leagues, we had to spend the money to get the talent. It was a big leap for us." The management team agreed to recruit at a much higher level than they had originally anticipated. And they found the marketing vice president they wanted in Richard Pauley, who was director of marketing and public relations at the University of Caifornia, Berkeley. "Richard brings a 'big league thinking' to our company," Schultz says. "Not just to the management team, but to the rank and file. He brings in a fresh perspective and asks probing questions that we otherwise wouldn't have considered." Now during product-development meetings, instead of just getting excited about the new products, the new marketing VP is asking: How does that affect our positioning? Does it fit with our strategy? What will the customers think? What is the market really telling us? What is our competition doing?"

Separating Sales and Marketing

To achieve consistent growth, companies must recognize the differences between sales and marketing. These are two separate functions in a business, and should be treated as such. The sales function consists of telemarketing, presentations, cold calls, and other methods to find new customers and close deals. The marketing function involves activities that are more strategic and analytical: market research, customer feedback, market positioning, market analysis, and strategic planning.

When firms stop growing, many CEOs interpret the problem as one of sales ineffectiveness. CEOs often respond by initiating more sales training, creating new sales systems, replacing sales managers, or pressuring salespeople. These approaches fail to get to the root of the problem. Although a strong sales organization is important for growing companies, the real constraint to growth often involves marketplace changes. Working harder to sell a market that has shifted in a new direction is unlikely to bring results. "It's like having the cannon, but firing it in the wrong direction," says one executive.

Step 3. Commit to Rigorous Practices of Market Research

Market research is highly correlated with growth and financial success in entrepreneurial firms. Market research involves gathering data from the marketplace that links a customer to a company's present and future performance. Good market research taps in to information relevant to strategic decision-making.

Growth companies invest substantially in market research, making it a corporate priority. These firms build systematic capabilities within their organizations that allows them to gather a consistent, steady stream of Market Intelligence. Nongrowth companies approach market research haphazardly, and invest little or no resources in this function. To them it is not a priority.

The first step in gathering market research is to clearly define the problem you are trying to solve, or the question you are trying to answer. This focuses your activities. The market research can then be conducted in many ways. Although it is entirely appropriate, hiring expensive consulting firms that use complex market research techniques is not always necessary. Data on your market can be obtained from a variety of sources, from as narrow a point of view as an individual customer, or as broad as looking at an entire industry.

Some starting places to get market research include annual reports (if the companies you are researching are publicly traded companies); competitors' speeches, press releases, and advertisements; libraries; trade groups; the Internet; customer focus groups; telephone surveys; and books and directories such as *Thomas Register*, and publications put out by Dun & Bradstreet, Standard & Poor's, Moody's, etc. For more resources, see Chapter 8.

Focus Groups and Telephone Surveys

Focus Groups

As Specialized Bicycle Components, of Morgan Hill, California, learned, focus groups are a good way to obtain customer feedback and plan for new products. The company, which was founded in 1974 and has revenues of more than $160 million, conducts about 10 focus groups a year involving 8 to 12 participants, and believes they are key to its success. Kaylie Pirie, director of market research, thinks there are several things a company can do to get the most out of each session.

"Ask a friend to play moderator," Pirie says. "It's hard for a CEO to ask neutral questions, especially when he or she is the advocate of an idea." (It's usually best for the friend to be from outside the company.) It's important to tell participants up-front that there are no right or wrong answers, that you're not there to form a consensus, and that they should speak up when they don't like something. It also helps to start with easy questions, so that everyone feels comfortable speaking—questions like "What brand of bike do you ride?" and "How many miles a week do you ride?"

"Good questions are usually open-ended, such as 'How did you go about selecting your last bike?'" says Pirie. "They force people to expand on their answers." And be sure to ask general questions, such as "What would your ideal bike be like?," before you start asking about details. If you show participants a product right at the beginning, they end up spending the session concentrating mostly on that.

Key questions to ask in focus groups include:

1. What are the key factors in your decision to use our products and services?

2. What were your expectations for our products and services—and to what degree have they been met?

3. What additional products or services would you like us to offer?

4. How is the quality of the product/service?

5. Please help us evaluate our overall process:
   - Marketing/sales
   - Manufacturing/operations
   - Customer service
   - Billing

6. What has been the most disappointing aspect of our product/service, and how do you think it could be corrected in the future?

7. What is the single most valuable aspect of our service/product?

8. Do you purchase from any of our competitors? Why?

(Source of questions: Bottom Line Consultants, © 1997)

Telephone Surveys

When Karen Scott got started in the mail-order baby products business, she put together her own focus group over the phone using the local newspaper. After clipping 250 birth announcements, Scott contacted the new moms, sent them surveys, and conducted phone interviews, asking what products young mothers sought. Based on the responses, Scott added more travel products at her company, Chelsea and Scott, located in Lake Bluff, Illinois. Ten years later, travel products are still top sellers at the $28 million company.

Step 4. Assess Marketplace Information Regularly

After gathering marketplace information, carefully assess it. Your company's strengths and weaknesses should be determined in relation to this information. The company's strengths should be leveraged to take advantage of growth opportunities; its weaknesses should be eliminated, or reduced. Only when a company acknowledges the strategies or practices that hold it back can it break free of them.

Kliklok-Woodman manufactures high-speed packaging systems used by food manufacturers such as Ore-Ida, Frito Lay, and Heinz. The company had grown to $50 million in annual sales, but revenues flattened out toward the mid-1980s. The market segments Kliklok was serving—high-end snack products, frozen foods, and baked goods—had matured. A wave of consolidations in the industry had brought a lessening in demand for new equipment.

During those first few years of flat sales, president Peter Black held annual retreats with his management team to discuss new growth strategies. After the meetings, managers promised to implement these ideas. But then by the time the next retreat rolled around, nothing had changed. "Management wasn't too concerned, because the margins were improving, so they felt pretty comfortable," Black explains. But he wanted to shake things up. "Finally, three years ago at our annual management meeting, I decided to put up some spreadsheets that showed our ten-year history, but I adjusted the numbers for inflation." With inflation accounted for, the numbers revealed that the business had been declining year after year. Black made the message clear: "We've been doing the same things for the last nine years, and it's not good enough anymore. It's time to challenge our basic assumptions about this business." The group then went about the task of redefining their business *according to the needs of the market.*

"We had stalled out because we had too narrow a view of what our business was, which prevented us from breaking out of the industries we historically had served," says Black. So, for the first time ever, the company did some serious analysis. Management looked at the company's strengths and weaknesses, assessed the competition, and then did market research to determine where the growth opportunities existed. For the first time, they set aside the money for a marketing development budget.

As a result of the analysis, management redefined its business. They no longer define it in terms of the industry they serve but rather in terms of their specialized engineering and technology. "We make vertical form-filled seal packaging," says Black. This new identity allows managers to see markets that had never been considered before. In the process, managers have become much closer to customers, establishing collaborative relationships with key accounts to fine-tune new technology, production, and strategy. "We can no longer just assume that we know our market," Black reflects. "We have entered entirely new industries that we had never worked in before, and we ask a lot of questions." The new markets include fresh vegetables, packaging of liquids, and semirigid containers. The company hasn't broken through to the next curve yet, but the management team is doing its homework and assessing it regularly. They are determined not to be blind-sided again.

Step 5. Make Strategic Decisions on the Basis of Market Intelligence

Consolidate Marketplace Intelligence so that strategic decisions are aligned with market realities. Many companies implement the first four steps of building Market Intelligence, but then don't act on this information to generate new strategies for growing and competing more effectively.

Growth companies take chances and try new approaches. They are open to innovations in their market concept, product development, distribution channels and market focus. Because they have accessed the relevant information from the marketplace, they are consistently making changes ahead of their competitors. Stalled companies never jettison their original market concept. They do business according to the same formula that gave them their success through Stage 2. These companies are stuck in patterns of behavior and find it difficult to do business differently.

IMPROVING YOUR MARKET INTELLIGENCE QUOTIENT (MIQ)

How smart is you company when it comes to Market Intelligence? Your company's Market Intelligence can by measured by the depth of your knowledge of the following factors:

1. Who your customers are
2. Your customers' wants and needs

3. Your customers' challenges and opportunities

4. Your competition

5. The market at large

If your company needs to build Market Intelligence, you must determine where to start. Use the following Market Intelligence factors to guide your acquisition of knowledge.

1. *Who* Your Customers Are

At the core of Market Intelligence is knowledge of the customer. To compete successfully, a business must acquire extensive knowledge about its customers' needs, wants, choices, and preferences, both now and in the future. This knowledge is the key to developing externally focused strategies for growth.

This process begins by defining who your customers are. A good test is to ask 10 different employees to describe your customer. How do they respond? Do you get blank stares? Do you receive a different answer from each employee? Do you get a description of your industry? Or do you find a specific profile being articulated that reveals an intimate understanding of a customer? The question of who are your customers must be thoroughly answered before your company can develop sound growth strategies.

As they grow, many companies lose a sense of who their customers are. These companies can define a broad category of customers, but they cannot pinpoint those who will have the greatest impact on the company's future success.

In determining who your customers are, identify specifically those who can contribute the most to future growth and profitability—those who are worth the most to your company in the future. Many companies' customer profiles reveal an 80-20 rule: 20 percent of their customers contribute to 80 percent of their sales and profits. Look at your company's customer base and see if there is a similar breakdown. These key customers are the ones that can teach you the most about future growth strategies.

2. Your Customers' Wants and Needs

For many growing companies, selling becomes the paramount corporate activity. Their attitude is that once customers are acquired, there is no need to spend any more time with them other than filling orders.

In these companies, customers become a business transaction—not part of a relationship.

A friend of mine, David, works in a 70-employee Midwest engineering-services firm that provides international architectural and structural engineering for pharmaceutical and food companies. David recently complained that the business was stalled, and that management was neglecting their clients. Many company contracts were two to three years in length, and required periodic reviews by the clients. Halfway through one $25 million contract, the clients' review process revealed a number of problems, including a lack of quality, service, and effective project management. David's firm failed to address these issues. After three requests for attention with no results, they took their business to a competing firm.

Instead of facing what had caused the clients' departure and working to correct the problems, management blamed the customers for the complaints—and now, the company is frantically looking for new customers to replace the one it lost. But David knows that this pattern of neglect will only lead to more and more such incidents.

This company is in trouble. Without changes in management's attitude toward customers it will fail. Unless a company understands and meets its customers' needs, it will be vulnerable to its competition. One of the most logical strategies for growth is to focus intensely on your current customers. The most loyal customers are also the most profitable. Research has documented that it is much more expensive to find a new customer than to keep existing ones. The key is to think of customers as participants in a long-term relationship rather than as another business transaction.

Customer Satisfaction

Today's customers are well educated, sophisticated, and demanding. They expect superior levels of quality and service, which are no longer seen as a luxury or a competitive advantage but *simply as the tickets that allow you to compete in the game.* Your business competes not only against your known competitors but also against companies such as Disney and Nordstrom, which are setting the standards for remarkable customer service. These service-focused firms have raised the bar in the public's mind regarding expectations for service. Once you have experienced Disney, or Nordstrom, then that becomes the standard by which you judge all other service experiences. If your company is not providing excellence in quality and service, you are vulnerable to competitors who do. High customer satisfaction is fundamental to business survival.

Rigorous customer feedback mechanisms must be built to assess and monitor customers' perceptions of quality and service. Informal discussions, or casual conversations from front-line employees and sales or customer service staff are inadequate methods of determining customer perceptions. If you don't know objectively how customers are viewing your company's performance according to *their* standards, you are operating in the dark.

The most common method for monitoring customer satisfaction is through customer feedback surveys. Since the mid-1980s, Makovsky & Co. has been keeping tabs on client relationships by asking account managers for written feedback. That practice has helped the 16-year-old New York City public-relations agency identify problems before its clients do. In 1992, the company founder, Ken Makovsky, started asking his customers for their input as well, using a detailed questionnaire. "I realized that our evaluations were too one-sided," says Makovsky. He wanted to measure clients' perceptions about the agency's ability to generate media results, manage a budget, and perform as a team. The survey asks customers pointed questions such as "Are we giving you your money's worth?" and also asks them about individual account team members.

Makovsky asks small clients for feedback once a year, whereas large, complex accounts are surveyed twice yearly. Everyone involved with the project receives a questionnaire and a letter of explanation. Makovsky & Co. team leaders typically follow up with a phone call to the roughly 50 clients to encourage them to complete the questionnaires. Makovsky estimates that 65 percent do so.

The survey process is time-consuming and sometimes painful, Makovsky says, but it has elicited candid feedback from customers. In the past, some problems were never brought to light until it was too late. For example, one client had worked with Makovsky & Co. for five years and then coldly invited the agency to rebid on the expired contract. The agency didn't get the bid, but Ken Makovsky did call the client—and discovered that the president had never liked the account manager. "A lot of clients won't pick up the phone and tell you that," says Makovsky.

"With the survey we found out some things we wouldn't have found out otherwise." For instance, about a staff member Makovsky considered a star, but who was panned by a client. Or about the assistant account executive whose contributions fell off the company's radar, but not the client's. "We didn't realize that she was so valuable," says Makovsky; he promoted her to account executive. It has also cleared up simple misunderstandings. In one case, an international client that was habitually late paying its bills needed the invoice rerouted through its U.S. division. Suddenly, 90 days turned into 30.

With an average of three client reviews coming in each month, Makovsky has set up a forum to handle the feedback. At a monthly meeting, teams meet with senior managers and a consultant to discuss the survey results. Three months later, the team reports back about how it is addressing problems. The results for the company have been an improved client-retention rate, up 20 percent from the pre-review years. And 22 percent of the company's $5.4 million in net revenues now come from client referrals.

3. Your Customers' Challenges and Opportunities

With customer feedback mechanisms in place, your company can now take the next step and begin to use more sophisticated Market Intelligence to drive company growth. Although customer feedback surveys provide valuable information regarding your product, quality, and service, these are just a *first* step. Customer feedback surveys typically rely on closed-ended questions designed by the management team to elicit a "yes" or "no" response. Or they may include a rating scale to grade quality or service. For most companies seeking customer feedback, this is where their efforts end. However, an entirely new level of strategic opportunities emerges when you start asking customers open-ended questions such as How are *you* doing? What does your future look like? What are your short- and long-term goals and strategies? What kinds of challenges are you facing? The answers provide your company with revealing strategic information and insights that can give you an enormous edge over your competitors.

Beyond Customer Satisfaction—Customer Collaboration

Customer collaboration, or strategic listening (a term used by Richard Whiteley and Diane Hessan in their book *Customer Centered Growth*), is a cutting-edge growth strategy concept. By collaborating with key customers and suppliers, a company discovers new opportunities to create unique value, develops "proprietary relationships," and stays one step ahead of customers and the competition. With this information, companies can anticipate and solve customers' problems in ways *customers may not have thought of or asked for.*

"We want to create products that are unknown to the customer, products that fulfill unspoken needs," say Mike Tsou, chief technical officer at Saturn Electronics and Engineering in Auburn Hills, Michigan, a $123 million supplier to the auto industry. This approach landed Saturn on the *Inc.* 500 list for six consecutive years (1991–1996) in an industry that is anything but hot. In 1990, Saturn was just an $8 million company.

Things in the auto industry used to be a lot simpler. The carmaker would hand the supplier a blueprint and say, "Give me a million of these parts, and make sure you build enough profit into your quote." It's nothing like that now. "Today you have to get in with the customer early on the front end," says Tsou. Saturn is currently designing parts for cars that won't appear in the showrooms for another four years.

Saturn's philosophy has been to integrate technology with marketing, which Tsou says "gives us a chance to drive the market." To create the necessary sense of surprise, Saturn must get as close as possible to its key customers.

Tsou joined Saturn after working General Motors for 30 years. He understands the culture and thinking at GM, one of Saturn's largest customers. Similarly, Nick Najmolhoda, now Saturn's executive vice-president of engineering, worked for many years with Chrysler, Saturn's largest customer. Meanwhile, Saturn CEO Wally Tsuha has cultivated close contacts at Ford. So for each of Saturn's three largest customers, which together account for 80 percent of sales, the company has a "point man" with close ties. As Tsou puts it, "We like to be able to talk to people at high levels in those companies."

But Tsou hasn't left it at that. He has replicated these close ties at the plant-manager level. Dennis Rainwater, the general manager of a Saturn plant in Oxford, Michigan, says, "We see our customers as often as three times a week." Pete Grim, who manages Saturn's plant in Rochester Hills, Michigan, adds, "We have to have a lot of on-site visibility at our customers' plants. Otherwise, they don't think we're serious about having an impact on their business."

Tsou says that by being so close to its customers Saturn knows what's "on their wish list" and from that can seize the design initiative. One proprietary product that resulted from a customer's wish list sits on the conference-room table in front of Rainwater. It's a small mechanical device called a direct-drive vent-window actuator. In plain English, it opens the rear window on a minivan. Alongside Saturn's actuator sits the Japanese part it recently displaced, which comes as two pieces connected by a cable. "Our actuator is a third the weight and half the cost. It's also easier to install, which saves money," notes Rainwater.

Saturn's actuator represents two years of research and development and a significant investment—with no guarantee that the customer would buy the product. To close the sale, Rainwater's division went the final mile by developing, at an additional cost of $100,000, a computerized "sound map" that tests parts for quietness, ensuring that they fall below a certain noise threshold. "We initiated that on our own," says Rainwater.

Saturn had met the customer's unspoken need. Rainwater says the customer (which wants to remain anonymous for competitive reasons) saw not just the elegance and the economy of the part but also the value added by the sound map. No other supplier had taken the initiative to test for noise to that extent. But, as Rainwater explains, "Noise is a big issue with our customers. They tell us that all the time." The company is already at work on the next-generation product, while the customer is now interested in having Saturn design other parts it can test on the sound map.

Adopt a clean slate when approaching customers. Put aside your preconceived ideas about customers and your tunnel vision about your own products and services, so that you can truly put yourself in the customer's shoes. Customers should be viewed as active participants in your company's growth strategies.

Robotron, based in Southfield, Michigan, manufactures welding equipment used by major auto and appliance manufacturers to control robots in their sheet-metal production facilities. The current owner, Len Brzozowski, was brought in by the board of directors in 1986 to shut down the business. Overseas competition, price cuts, and the demands for quality standards had taken its toll. Robotron had lost money for 10 years in a row—in 1985 it lost $1.8 million on sales of $9 million. As he went about his task, Brzozowski became impressed by the employees' commitment, knowledge, and skill. He decided to see if he could salvage the company by asking customers what they needed, and possibly find opportunities to forge new markets or make the company more competitive.

Brzozowski took his top three managers with him to visit the plants of the company's best customers. At each plant, for several days they would walk the plant floor and talk to supervisors, managers, and front-line employees who used their welding machines, who would tell them about their problems and challenges

As Brzozowski and his team listened they realized they could offer solutions. By speaking with their customers, they found gaps in the competitive marketplace *that no one else was filling.* For instance, many older, more seasoned engineers had left the workforce (particularly in the auto industry) during the downsizing of the eighties. This had left a gap in technical knowledge on the plant floors. Robotron had a wealth of technical expertise and experience to offer. Brzozowski began sending his engineers to customer plant sites to help solve technical difficulties and train plant employees. Robotron now runs a training business for its customers, including the development of an interactive training software system for workers on the shop floor.

Since those initial visits, Robotron's revenues have grown to $27 million and the company has achieved solid profits, a fiercely loyal customer base, award-winning technology innovations, and a workforce that outperforms the industry averages by 50 percent. All because the CEO decided to ask the customers what they wanted.

Client Advisory Board

The key to customer collaboration is dialogue. One of the best forums for generating dialogue for strategic listening is a customer or client advisory board that brings your best customers together regularly to provide your company with raw information about their (the customers') current challenges and future strategies. The advisory-board approach allows for confidential discussion to take place in an open, non-selling environment.

These boards have many other benefits. They build loyalty among your best customers, who are genuinely flattered when asked to participate in such strategic meetings. They also generate authentic customer feedback because the board members discuss their problems and concerns *in a context unconnected from buying your products or services.* In such an environment, market-focused ideas and insights for new innovations, services, or products emerge easily. This can take your company in new directions and reveal previously unnoticed opportunities.

Getting Started. To assemble a client advisory board, select a handful of your top customers—those that are the most influential and represent target markets and areas where your company is strategically committed. Selection criteria are the following: Which customers will we learn the most from? And which customers can we leverage the most to grow market share and increase profitability? *Remember, this is not a sales call, and should not be perceived as a sales-driven event by the customer, even indirectly.* You are getting your customers together to discuss *their* business issues, *their* industry, *their* strategies, etc.

Always prepare open-ended questions that will initiate roundtable discussion among the customer advisory board. Here are some sample questions:

- What trends do you see coming in your industry that will impact your business?
- What will be better and different in your company three to five years from now?
- What are the three to four key goals you want to achieve in the next two years?
- How will you know when you've achieved those objectives?
- What are the biggest challenges that may prevent you from achieving those results?
- What do you think are the most important issues your clients or customers are dealing with?
- How do you create a competitive advantage for your customers?
- What would your customers say is the most valuable service you provide?
- Whom do you consider to be your competition?
- What makes you better or different from your competitors?

Add questions relevant to your business or industry.

When Your Customers Are Competitors. It stands to reason that some of your customers will be in the same business and will, in fact, be competitors. A roundtable setting is not feasible when some key customers are competitors. With these customers, try this exercise one-on-one. Use a standard template of questions to gather feedback so you can compare responses in an organized way. Track the responses and analyze them to determine whether common themes emerge that indicate new trends or changing market conditions.

The frequency of meetings with your client advisers is up to you and them. Once a year, once a quarter, once a month are all fine. Regardless of frequency, you should receive strategic information from your customers regularly. This helps you anticipate changing conditions. Since intimacy is vital for success, groups should not be larger than eight individuals.

When inviting customers to participate in this activity, remember the following points:

1. Make it clear that this is not a sales-related event.

2. Describe your interest in understanding the customer's point of view, and stress the validity of your customer's insights and knowledge of the marketplace.

3. Let them know that this has been a highly selective process. Explain to them why they have been chosen (you are strategically committed to that industry and its customers in the future; they are recognized as leaders within the industry).

On-site Customer Observation

Another example of strategic listening involves learning about customers by observing them at their facilities. Again, stay far away from selling. Just watch how customers interact with your product or service. By studying them in their everyday business environment and watching their experiences, frustrations, and challenges, you will see many opportunities for improvements and innovations.

Take the case of Lantech, a packaging systems firm in Louisville, Kentucky. Pat Lancaster, its founder, has always aspired to keep Lantech the industry leader. Lancaster consistently looks to be one step ahead of his competitors. He makes frequent visits to his customers' facilities to watch them use Lantech packaging systems.

On one occasion he was standing in the shipping area of a customer. Lancaster noticed that a woman using the Lantech packaging system kept bending down to hit a switch. As Lancaster observed her constant bending, he started thinking, "That must hurt her back after a full day's work. I wonder if she calls in sick frequently because of back pain? I wonder if the company's workers' compensation would be affected by this?" The answer to both of these questions was yes.

Back at Lantech, Lancaster relayed his observations to his management team. Three weeks later, Lancaster returned to the customer with an innovation on the packaging system: An operator could now *hit the switch with her foot* rather than bending down. The system was improved, workers were happier, and workers' compensation costs fell. Would the customer have asked Lancaster to make this improvement? Probably not. Would the woman on the front lines ever demand a change in the system to eliminate bending down constantly? Unlikely. By being available and paying close attention to the customer, Lantech continuously makes innovations and maintains its position as industry leader.

Lexus is another company that illustrates the power of on-site observation. In designing its sales and service systems, Lexus hired anthropologists to study human behavior in the car sales rooms. The scientists saw how customers became uncomfortable when approached by salespeople, leading Lexus to design sales centers where customers could view the cars on their own. Salespeople became involved only when and if customers initiated the conversations. Lexus has become number one in customer satisfaction, ahead of BMW, Mercedes, and Porsche.

How familiar are you with the customer's use of your products or services? Do you *really know* what it's like on the "other side"? A passive mode of strategic listening allows you to pick up on subtle frustrations or problems that are being experienced by the people who are using your products and services on a day-to-day basis. Once they have been identified, you can determine whether there are opportunities to make innovations and changes that truly improve the lives of your customers.

Strategic listening offers more knowledge about your market, your customers, and the future needs of these customers than any survey. That information allows you to establish a collaborative or consultative relationship, and to act as a problem-solving resource for your customers. You consistently get creative new insights and ideas that fuel innovation. Instead of reacting to the market or the competition, strategic listening allows you to drive the market.

4. Your Competition

Another aspect of Market Intelligence is gathering information about your competitors. The more you know about your competitors' strengths, weaknesses, strategies, and financial condition the better equipped you will be to develop competitive strategies. This information enables your company to understand your unique position in the market, and to capitalize on your competitors' weaknesses as well as on gaps in the marketplace. Your strategies can focus on high-leverage opportunities that are difficult for your competitors to replicate.

Trade groups, customers, suppliers, and employees who have been hired from competitors provide sources for understanding the competition. If your competitors are public companies, information can be obtained from annual reports.

Craig Stouffer, CEO of Mobius Computer Corp., gathers competitive information by using the Internet. "You can post a question on the newsgroups about products or systems, and 4,500 people respond with their experiences." A slight exaggeration, yes, but there's no question that the number of people you can reach on the Internet is astonishing. When Craig first logged on, about a year and a half ago, there were some 8,500 newsgroups. Now there are nearly twice that many. Methodically reading through all the subject descriptions, he came up with just over 200 newsgroups on topics pertinent to his business. These days he only has time to read the postings in five or six groups each day, but having gone through the huge list once, he can now cut to the chase with the utmost efficiency.

Many of the resources that businesspeople like Stouffer are mining online—such as the inside scoop on competitors from real customers—weren't accessible to them previously in any form. "There's information available now on the Internet that's never been available anywhere," says Trey Seitz, formerly director of operations at Competitive Intelligence International in Chicago, a consulting firm that specializes in digging up industry dirt. "The newsgroups are a good place to get information anonymously from experts, and on mailing lists you can find competitors and their customers."

Getting the goods from the Internet is not always that simple. But investing a few hours each week in finding useful information is the only way to test the possibilities.

Predicasts' Overview of Markets and Technology (PROMT) is a one-stop database for public and private company information and industry information found in print media, such as trade journals, newspapers, magazines, and industry reports. Most main-branch libraries in metropolitan areas have access to PROMT, which you can surf using a company's name, key word, standardized industrial classification (SIC) code, and much more.

Also available in many libraries is *Ward's Business Directory of U.S. Private and Public Companies* and Dun and Bradstreet's *Million Dollar Directory*, which provide vital intelligence on competitors, such as sales figures and the names of a company's chief officers. But to put flesh on those bones, you'll need Dun's Market Identifier, a database you can search by SIC (up to eight digits), region, sales volume, number of employees, Zip code, and more.

Ward's Manufacturing U.S.A. and Service Industry U.S.A. resources go a step beyond Dun and Bradstreet's by offering payroll and production numbers, 10 years of sales, and key ratios, such as the number of employees, or the amount of payroll, per establishment. You can also get numbers on materials consumed by specific companies, which allows you to identify emerging market opportunities. For more resources, see Chapter 8.

5. The Market at Large

In addition to getting feedback from individual customers, it is important to keep up with trends and changes in the market at large. Individual customers present a "micro" view of what's going on in your industry; the "macro" perspective allows your company to stay abreast of issues or changes that may impact your business in the future. Every business or industry is experiencing constant change, driven by new technology, breakthroughs in science, changing demographics, social and political shifts, or globalization.

For industry news and views, publications such as Dun and Bradstreet *Industry Norms* and Standard and Poor's *Industry Surveys* give snapshots of many industries and the key ratios and figures for the major players in each. Also check the U.S. Commerce Department's *U.S. Industrial Outlook* for new legislation or new products in your market and your sector's long-term prospects.

The importance of understanding future trends in the marketplace cannot be overstated. The proliferation of books by futurists predicting the state of the world in the future and interpreting the overwhelming amount of information available to us attests to the increasing attention given to this area. Yogi Berra may have said it best: "The future ain't what it used to be." The pace of change will continue to increase. These days, the CEO and management of companies that want to grow to the next level must become their own futurists. In *Competing for the Future,* Gary Hamel and C. K. Prahalad state that if a leader cannot clearly articulate the five or six fundamental trends that most threaten the firm's continued success, he or she is not in control of the firm's destiny.

What are the *three* trends that will most impact the future of your industry? Jot them down here.

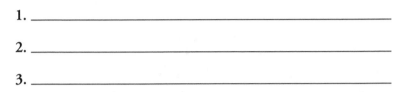

The information you just wrote down cannot be ignored. By your own admittance, this is extremely important strategic information that must be explored, researched, monitored, and understood. Why? Because it represents the future of your business. Whoever commits the time and energy required to understand and influence these forces will be in the best position to recognize new opportunities and capitalize on them.

CHAPTER 4

Strategic Leadership

STRATEGIC LEADERSHIP CONCERNS THE ROLE OF THE CEO, and how that role affects a company's growth. Although it is an area of critical importance, business owners often struggle with Strategic Leadership because it involves managing themselves as well as the business. The key to successful leadership is this: As a company grows, the owner must also grow.

The role of the CEO in a growing, privately held company is unique. You, the entrepreneur, are accountable to no one, yet the fate of the entire enterprise rests on your shoulders. There is no one evaluating your performance, or giving feedback on how well you are doing your job. In fact, many entrepreneurs started their own companies for this very reason—they wanted to be their own boss. The experience of being completely independent of a higher authority certainly has its benefits and rewards, but it has an inherent down side: There is no one you can *talk* to—no one who really *understands* what it's like to be in your position. Regardless of this lack of guidance, you must make decisions every day for which there are no precedents, like what kinds of people to hire; how much money to borrow; what strategies are most appropriate; which technology to utilize. All are complex, dynamic issues that keep changing over time, forcing the CEO constantly to enter new territory.

There is no safety net to catch you if you slip. The success or failure of a business enterprise falls squarely on the shoulders of the leader. An entrepreneur's drive, passion, and aspiration are applauded when business is good, but if business performance is on the skids, the finger always points to the entrepreneur and his lack of good judgment. Talk to those who have presided over the demise, or near death, of their fast-growing entities and they'll almost never list external factors as the critical culprits. Most of the failures of growth companies are due to internal problems—which, of course, inevitably come back to the leader. At the end of the day, all the responsibility, blame, victory, and praise go to the leader, whatever the outcome of the business. Given the link between the entrepreneur and the success of the business, it is critical to assess the role of the CEO in gauging an organization's ability to grow.

Some would argue that entrepreneurs are, by definition, mavericks, so this talk about leadership skills need not apply. Their companies are successful because they are willing to take risks and are insistent on doing everything their own way. No doubt this cavalier style is certainly appropriate during the early stages of growth, but when the company moves up the curve to Stage 2, what happens? The business becomes more complex. The stakes are higher. There are more responsibilities— to employees, customers, and investors. The notion of "winging it," which was so attractive in the early days of business growth, is now a risky proposition because of these pressing obligations. As the company grows, the entrepreneur must make a transition. But this time, the skills required to lead a company from one level of growth to the next are generally more strategic and managerial than technical, sales, or operational.

Stage 1 and Stage 2 companies are initially successful not because of the entrepreneur's great leadership capabilities, but because of his operational, sales, or technical skills. How else does a business get started and make it through the first hurdles of growth? The computer systems expert starts a consulting business. The engineer creates an engineering firm. The graphic designer founds a design house. And the sales champion launches any business—because whatever the product or service is, he can sell it. Rarely does a new business enterprise get launched simply because some entrepreneur somewhere says, "I'd love to be a terrific CEO. Hmm, what kind of business can I start to be a good leader?" Once the business is launched, however, the skills required to lead a company from one level of growth to the next are generally more strategic and managerial than technical, sales, or operational.

Hedy Holmes, the CEO and the top salesperson of Hedy Holmes Staffing Service, in Stockton, California, recalls that she was "becoming overwhelmed," as her company rode up the growth curve. "Strategic thinking was going by the wayside. Accounting and technology were neglected. Customer service was suffering. My employees were saying, 'Well, I guess the only thing that matters around here is sales.'" It wasn't until she was on the brink of burnout that Hedy relented and hired a top salesperson. This enabled her to concentrate on building the company for the long term.

The key requirement for the CEO in getting to the next level is to make the transition from an owner-manager to a strategic leader. I have spoken with many entrepreneurs who literally wake up one day and realize that the role they have always played in the past, as the lead technical or salesperson, will not be effective for the company's future growth. When this realization strikes, they work hard at stretching themselves to become better leaders—even if some are more comfortable and familiar with that previous role. Marc Albin, CEO of Albin Engineering in Sunnyvale, California, is an entrepreneur who struggled with the transition from engineer to CEO. Albin had a burgeoning computer systems consulting firm on his hands, which had grown from nothing to $6 million in three short years. But Albin knew that taking on the role of a true CEO would mean acting, thinking, and behaving differently than he did as an engineer.

"I didn't want to fall back in to my old habits," Albin says, "and I wanted to come up with a way to remind myself that I was not the same person any more." How did Albin remind himself that he was a CEO now? He parted his hair on the other side of his head. Simple, yes, but effective for Mr. Albin. "Every time I scratch my head, I remember that I'm not an engineer anymore," Albin says. "It's a physical way of doing something different, and it reminds me to carry on my new role as a new person and to think differently." After 35 years of parting his hair on the other side, the new hairstyle is an ongoing reminder of the professional and personal growth ahead.

Unlike Marc Albin, other business owners deny that their lack of leadership skills is a bottleneck to future growth, and blame external or internal factors if the company experiences problems. Putting the problems on someone or something else is a lot easier than looking in the mirror and facing one's own limitations and need for improvement. The ability to critically assess one's own leadership abilities is a difficult, challenging issue, on both a personal and professional level. But it must be addressed.

SO WHAT *IS* THE CEO'S JOB?
THE LEADERSHIP ROLE IN A GROWING COMPANY

The CEO's job, in a nutshell, is to create the company's future by setting forth a clear and compelling direction that is communicated to all employees, then to motivate and lead everyone toward that destination. The CEO's ability to provide clear direction, delegation, decision-making, and long-term planning are the core elements of sound leadership, and are all skills that must be developed in the CEO as the company grows. Those skills are not, naturally acquired abilities that are automatically vouchsafed to every entrepreneur. As a company grows and evolves, so must the leader.

As the business grows and becomes more complex, more time and energy is required of the CEO to think strategically and to prepare for the company's future. But the business's daily operations continue to demand attention.

How much time do you spend on planning for the future? Think back over the past week. How did you spend your time? How much of what you did was reaction to the world around you, compared with proactively determined priorities and actions? Do you even know what your priorities should be?

To help you answer this, look at the activities listed below. They are divided into two categories: Future-Related/Strategic Activities, and Day-to-Day Operational Activities. For each activity listed, estimate what percentage of your time you generally spend on it. Try to be precise enough so that the total comes out to 100 percent (add some activities if you have to, and assign them to either of the two categories). Then add up the percentage for each area. The total for both categories together should be 100 percent. Compare the amount of time you spend on activities that revolve around thinking and planning for your company's future with that spent on operational activities.

ANALYSIS: STRATEGIC LEADERSHIP

Future-Related/Strategic Activities (Percent of Time Spent)

___% Financing (meeting with banks, investors, drawing up business plans for financing)

___% Formal strategic planning

___% Attending industry-relevant conferences and trade shows

___% Establishing strategic alliances/relationships/networking

___% Reading journals, magazines, Internet sites related to your industry

___% Meeting with key customers to discuss their future strategies

___% Developing and mentoring management's professional skills

Day-to-Day Operational Activities (Percent of Time Spent)

___% Dealing with crisis situations

___% Taking customer orders

___% Developing proposals

___% Managing people

___% Selling

___% Technical activities (i.e., graphic design, writing code)

TOTAL: ___% (SHOULD EQUAL 100 PERCENT)

Fill in the blanks in the following statements.

Last week I spent _____ percent of my time on strategic activities and _____ percent of my time on operational activities.

Last month I spent _____ percent of my time on strategic activities and _____ percent of my time on operational activities.

Last year I spent _____ percent of my time on strategic activities and _____ percent of my time on operational activities.

This quiz gives you a baseline to evaluate the level of Strategic Leadership that you currently exercise.

The CEO of a growth firm should spend at least 25 percent of his time on strategic activities. Some CEOs have structured their organizations so they spend 100 percent of their time on strategic activities. This is not feasible for every entrepreneur. It depends on how far along you are on the growth curve and the depth of your management team.

Dan Maude is CEO of Beacon Application Services, an *Inc.* 500 company based in Framingham, Massachusetts. It provides information-systems consulting to large companies, primarily around implementation of Peoplesoft applications (financial and human resources). Maude knows his company has terrific growth prospects, but when the company hit $4 million in sales in 1996, he no longer wanted to manage the business himself. Given the accelerated pace of change in the industry, he believed that his time would be best spent in the marketplace rather than in daily operations. That would allow him to anticipate trends in technology and determine what would be the next wave of hot information systems for corporate America. Maude realized that he could not discover the answer if he was busy managing a consulting firm of 40 people.

So Maude hired a chief operating officer (COO) to take on the day-to-day management of the firm. The candidate for the job had worked with him at a previous employer, so he knew she would be exactly the right fit. She also happened to be his wife. Madeline took over the operations and with great skill has tuned up the business in a way that Maude never would have been able to. Maude is strategic leader 100 percent of the time—charting the new territory, keeping up with technology trends through industry news and trade shows, managing the unique cultural aspects of the business, considering strategies that will make his company more competitive—with very little involvement in operations. And Beacon Application continues to grow (projected 1998 sales: $12 million).

Being CEO of a growing company means that you will continually reach points where you find yourself at the very edge of your comfort level. Maybe the business has grown far beyond what you thought possible? Maybe you feel more comfortable as a technical person than dealing with people? Perhaps you worry that you are in over your head? The key to successful leadership in a growth company is the CEO's ability to grow and change and to provide a role model to the rest of the company of personal and professional development.

THE STORY OF MATS HERSTRONNER—CAN THIS CEO HANDLE MORE GROWTH?

AGV Products builds automated guided vehicles and related products for material handling. Its robotlike forklift machines are installed in plants like Home Depot's distribution center, where AGV's machines reduce manpower needs and increase controls. Or they can be found in situations where machines are better suited to do the material handling than humans are, like unloading disassembled warheads that contain uranium, or handling Kodak film that requires handling in total darkness. Business was booming, and with an average sale of $1,000,000 per client, the growth curve was looking impressive. But the CEO, Mats Herstronner, felt that he was getting in over his head. "I'm just an engineer by trade," he said. "I've never run a business before." He knew the business was quickly heading far beyond its current $4 million in sales, but Herstronner was concerned that he didn't have the skill to lead his company.

Herstronner decided he needed some guidance, and engaged a business adviser to assess his situation. The analysis revealed that although AGV Products was developing a solid reputation in the industry and had strong growth potential, Herstronner himself was potentially a weak link in terms of the company's ability to handle future growth. He was a great engineer who knew the technical aspects of installing the computer-driven machines better than anyone else in his company. He was also a great salesperson, able to sell large, complicated systems because of his extensive knowledge. Those were the very traits that had paved the way for AGV's initial success. But now those were no longer the most important traits he could offer the company.

Herstronner had hired highly skilled employees to handle technical engineering, project management, and sales, but they were constantly annoyed by his incessant need to be involved in their every decision. This meddling behavior was perpetuated by Herstronner's insistence that he personally maintain the title of project manager and senior systems engineer, as well as president. He had written himself into the organizational chart at three different levels. This was interpreted by the employees as a lack of trust in their doing their jobs. Even though the business was growing and skilled people had been hired, Herstronner was having a difficult time letting go of what he always knew best: being an engineer. Instead of forging ahead into the role of strategic leader, Herstronner instinctually resorted to an intense level of involvement in daily operations because it was most familiar and comfortable for him.

The results of the consultant's analysis focused primarily on Herstronner's need to make a transition from engineer-entrepreneur to CEO of a professionally managed firm. Specifically, Herstronner needed to redefine his role in the company as CEO, complete with job description, and reorganize the business to ensure that he was able to carry out his duties. This involved establishing a true management team that would further remove him from the details of the work and included a director of sales and marketing and a director of project management. Herstronner would continue in an administrative capacity, but work harder at building and developing the managers rather than doing everything himself. This meant holding weekly management meetings and getting them involved in strategic planning and professional development.

Knowing that this leap from engineer to CEO would be difficult, the consultant also encouraged Herstronner to get exposed to other CEOs of small growth companies who were dealing with the same kinds of issues. This would provide him with camaraderie and mentorship that had been missing, and help him to change his view of himself by associating with and learning from others who had successfully made that transition.

Over the next year Herstronner transformed himself and his company. He has joined a local CEO roundtable group where he learns a great deal about growth issues and has ongoing support and advice from other CEOs. He has participated in the Harvard Business School's Executive Management program, which brings in CEOs for three weeks at a time every three years for intensive leadership training. He has familiarized himself with leading business books. He has attended an *Inc.* conference on financing strategies. In the meantime, AGV's sales have doubled, and Herstronner is excited about the continuing prospects for new growth because he knows he can handle it.

Herstronner has made a conscious effort to stretch himself beyond his comfort level in order to prepare his company for future growth. By removing himself from the details of the project management and sales activities, he now can focus on structural and strategic issues that will have a far-reaching impact on the business.

Unfortunately, some other entrepreneurs do not take quite so much initiative to develop themselves as leaders. But many resources are available to business owners who are interested in professional growth, such as business conferences, leadership seminars, and regional CEO groups. There are many qualified business consultants and coaches who can act as challenging mentors. Even brushing up on the vast supply of business books can help expand the leader's thinking and provide a source of new ideas.

All CEOs should utilize these resources to establish their own professional development plans and avoid getting caught in an insular environment. Exposure to other CEOs and companies outside of your own environment is a key to good leadership and corporate growth. Entrepreneurs often get so intensely focused on their own business that they become isolated. Sharing your successes and challenges with peers can provide a level of support, accountability, and perspective that is reinvigorating.

For Marc Albin, spending time with other CEOs has totally transformed his outlook on both his business and his role as a CEO. "I'm an engineer by training," Albin says. "I can solve very complicated technical problems, but I'm into something completely different now."

He is referring, of course, to his position as CEO of Albin Engineering. Located in the heart of Silicon Valley, he gets dizzy contemplating the growth opportunities that are still to be taken. "If I had all the people and infrastructure I needed, I could take over the industry," he says. But he is trying to remain level-headed and manage his company's growth carefully.

Part of that cautious approach involves evaluating himself as CEO—critiquing his own strengths, weaknesses, and areas for improvement. But he had no reference point. "I woke up one day and realized I was a CEO now instead of an engineer. I had a few frightful moments because I felt like I was in dark tunnel." Some of that darkness was caused by his lack of knowledge of business and of exposure to other growth companies.

A turning point came for Albin in 1997 when he attended *Inc.* magazine's CEO Symposium, a four-day conference designed exclusively for leaders of small, fast-growth companies like Albin's. "I really wanted to be a good CEO, and I figured I could learn a lot from talking to these other CEOs and finding out what made each of them successful." Albin's experience with the symposium shone a great deal of light into his dark tunnel. "I realize now that being a CEO doesn't mean I have to know how to *do everything*." Now Albin tries to organize his time and energy around activities that are most productive for both him and his company. He's recruiting for a sales manager and vice-president of operations so he can deal with the higher-level strategic issues for the company's growth—like how to take over the industry.

SOUNDING BOARDS

Board of Directors

A board of directors or advisers can be a great source of outside perspective and will prevent CEOs from behaving in an insulated manner. It can provide some baseline of accountability that is often missing with entrepreneurs. Whether it's an informal advisory committee or a formal board with outside directors, it can help owners of growing companies to mature, build strategic alliances, and gain access to capital.

Doug Mellinger knows why he has an advisory board and a board of directors: to save him from himself. Mellinger founded his now $62 million software company, PRT Group Inc., in New York City in 1989, when he was just two years out of college. Early on, with $4 million in revenues, he went to his advisers with a plan to open 10 offices around the United States in one year. Since he lacked the financial resources and the management to do it, they advised against his plan. Today he's grateful that he followed their advice. "Entrepreneurs are the most dangerous creatures if left to their own devices," Mellinger explains. He credits his advisers with much of his professional development and the company's success. Two advisory-board members regularly give him and other key managers reading assignments and send them to leadership seminars. "There's a lot to be said for gray hairs," says Mellinger.

Many entrepreneurs avoid forming a group of advisers because they do not know where to look for expertise and lack the nerve to ask for help. When Mellinger started his business, he didn't let fear of rejection stop him from cold-calling the top executives in America for guidance. "I was a bulldog who wouldn't go away. I was so determined to get these guys to help me," he says. Mellinger used his experience as the cofounder of an association for collegiate entrepreneurs as a starting point to ask for advice about his start-up. "Very senior people get bombarded all day by people wanting to sell them something," he says. "They don't get hit up by people who just want advice."

Of the 40 or so executives he called, 15 agreed to meet with him for half an hour. Then he networked through seasoned executives like the chairman of a multi-billion-dollar company whom he'd met briefly through his entrepreneurial group. Mellinger asked people he admired to be his mentors and sit on either his board of directors or his advisory board. His tenacity has been rewarded: PRT's boards have included the chief information officers of several *Fortune* 1,000 companies.

Frequently Asked Questions About Boards

What if my board members think I'm an idiot? One common reservation about bringing in outside advisers is the fear of looking foolish. Ironically, that's the point of having an advisory board. "If you don't show them what your weaknesses are, they can't help you," says Doug Mellinger.

Patty DeDominic, the CEO of Los Angeles–based PDQ Personnel Services, remembers feeling sheepish at her first advisory-board meeting. After assembling a high-powered group of local executives to advise her staffing company, she discovered that her senior people had underprepared for the meeting. "Their reports lacked substance," she says. "It was apparent to all of us that if we had put more into the meeting, we would have gotten more out of it." Now that PDQ has $20 million in sales, DeDominic talks to her advisers monthly and sends them written company updates twice a year. At semiannual meetings, senior managers give presentations that include detailed financial information and specific details about key problems. The result? Better advice.

How should I use their time? Focus on important issues—and don't expect a cheering squad. When NetEdge Systems Inc. was in its infancy, CEO Al Bender asked his formal board of directors for possible solutions to a persistent difficulty. Then he took action, just in time for the next meeting. "I expected applause," says Bender, whose Research Triangle Park, N.C. company makes telecommunications equipment. "Instead they said, 'That's great. Let's get to the next problem.' They didn't fly 3,000 miles to tell us what a great job we were doing."

If I build it, will they come? Getting high-powered execs to sign on is one thing. Getting them to show up for the meetings is another. "The problem is, you can never pay them what they're worth," says Rick Stewart, the CEO of $30 million Frontier Cooperative Herbs, in Norway, Iowa, a distributor of spices and other products. So Stewart tries to make the quarterly meetings of his formal board fun. Since the five outside members have to fly in, Stewart hosts the meetings in appealing locations, like Boulder and the Bahamas—and he pays spouses' expenses, too. The night before, board members are taken out to dinner and later to, say, a comedy or blues club. To keep them happy during the rest of the year, Stewart sends them monthly shipments of Frontier products. "They should feel pampered," he says.

How much should I pay board members? This varies a great deal, depending on how often they meet—once a quarter, or once a month, or twice a year—and whether they have formal or informal responsibilities. Compensation can range from $2,500 to $5,000 a day at the high end to the kind of compensation Rick Stewart provides: dinner at a good restaurant in a vacation spot and personal gifts.

Informal Advisory Groups

Despite the advantages of having a formal or an informal board, some entrepreneurs don't want to spend time recruiting members, planning agendas, and luring advisers to meetings. An alternative: Some busy entrepreneurs are turning to peer advisory groups, in which local businesspeople meet regularly with a facilitator and help one another solve problems. These informal advisory groups are an increasingly common phenomenon.

Bill Macon worked hard to recreate one of the beloved benefits he'd left behind in his previous life: the rigorous system of strategic planning he had learned at Emerson Electric, a $10 billion manufacturer of electrical products. By tutoring a group of his peers in Emerson's planning methods, he hoped to revive for himself the part of the process he missed most since he'd bought his own company, Macon Electric Coil, three years earlier: the challenging exchange of ideas and, perhaps most important, the security that comes with knowing that if your plan is half-baked, someone will convincingly call you on it. It didn't work that way in his own $2 million business. "I have thirty-five employees," says Macon, "and I've never had a bad idea when I've made a presentation to them."

Macon believed that if he could teach Emerson's strategic-planning methods to his peers, he would recreate for himself the safety net he'd had at that company: they would give him praise when he deserved it, but they would also tell him when he was screwing up, because he would teach them how.

Macon started the learning process with three other CEOs, using his own company's numbers on three charts that broke down sales, profit and loss, and return on capital. By the end of the evening, he knew he was onto something. "Together, we all noticed that my forecast showed the company growing aggressively in years one and two, and then in years three, four, and five, we were just milking it," recalls Macon. "The forecast was based on the business that was in the pipeline, but we hadn't added any significant business. That opened my eyes to the fact that it's not too early to start thinking about the next step." As a result, Macon is now deciding whether to expand his core business or to consider an acquisition—both strategies that will keep the company growing. True, he eventually would have recognized the plan's flaws on his own, but he came away from that meeting with a lot more than just solid business advice. "It was the first time since I'd left Emerson that I was able to use that skill with people who really appreciated the significance of it," Macon says. "And it felt great." "In a small company, you spend a lot of time dealing with mundane tasks," says Macon. "But this is a complex process that makes me and the others think at a higher level than we do ninety percent of the time."

LEADERSHIP CHALLENGE ANALYSIS: HOW "EXPOSED" ARE YOU?

Take a moment to rate your level of exposure and involvement with professional development.

In the past 12 months have you:

_____ attended a conference on leadership?

_____ participated in an executive management program (usually sponsored by an academic institution)?

_____ attended a business conference?

_____ participated in a local CEO roundtable or peer advisory group?

_____ hired a personal business coach?

_____ established a mentor relationship with a respected adviser?

_____ met with a board of directors specifically for your company?

If you have not checked at least three boxes, then you are underexposed and possibly are leading your business from an isolated, insular environment. That may be fine—if you don't plan on growing your company. Otherwise, you may want to use these activities to create a professional development plan for yourself.

THE IMPORTANCE OF LETTING GO

As companies grow they often exceed the CEO's ability to manage them. The business complexities increase substantially with growth, yet many entrepreneurs have a difficult time letting go because their control over every decision was crucial to the company's original success. But if this behavior continues when the company is larger, the CEO becomes a bottleneck, seriously constraining the business's growth potential. When the CEO is out of the office, people can't make decisions because they are afraid that they will be second-guessed or overruled when the CEO returns. Even though some may have been hired or promoted to management positions, the CEO insists on knowing and approving every decision. Authority and accountability of individual employees or managers is indistinct—no one is certain whom they are accountable to, other than the CEO. The dependent behavior only reinforces the CEO's belief that he has to be involved in the details of the business. When this happens, trust erodes and talented people, unable to function under such undermining circumstances, leave. Even though the managers are anxious to do their job, to prove themselves and to perform well, they are frustrated by the hovering CEO. Managers often find it difficult to voice this complaint to the CEO so he remains oblivious to the problems he is causing.

Those who try to maintain a firm grip on the business operations after it has grown beyond their capacity to manage it will eventually become tired, burned-out, and overwhelmed. The original spark that drove them to launch the business is gone. It's not fun anymore. Instead, every day is filled with solving problems, settling disputes, and managing crises. The CEO's need to control everything leads to the organization's being entirely *out of* control.

The Cost of Being in Control

Jan Pringle, the cofounder of Pringle, Dixon, Pringle, an Atlanta ad agency, is a case in point. She was diagnosed with a stress disorder after being physically carried from her office desk to the hospital late one night several years ago. The doctors concluded that she needed to take an extended leave of absence from her company. Back at home, she lay down on the living room couch and thought to herself, "I just want to die. I don't care if I ever return to my company."

But a year later she did. And ever since, Pringle has wrestled with one of the toughest questions a leader ever faces: Has her company outgrown her? "This isn't about whether the widget I make is outdated," she explains quietly. "It's about whether *I* am outdated."

The company grew in the 1980s to be one of Atlanta's hottest ad shops, and at its peak was posting impressive billings of $50 million, an annualized growth rate of 20 percent. The creative awards given in the ad industry, the ADDYs and Effies, were piling up. But Jan Pringle and her partner-husband, Jim, seemed unable to share credit with other employees. Although their employees played an integral part in key campaigns, many felt unappreciated, and many left. "In advertising you're only as good as your people," says Jeane Cartwright Aydlotte, an advertising account executive who was one of those who left. "The talent PDP assembled was incredible, and the talent they let go was equally incredible." With annual employee turnover running at 50 percent, employees allege that clients felt a lack of continuity, and many took their business elsewhere. In the mid-eighties, Aydlotte recalls, PDP's clientele was turning over at least every two years; the industry norm was seven.

Pringle, however, considered herself to be a leader able to do it all, juggling many balls in the air at the same time. Her day typically began at 7 A.M., with breakfast with either a client or one of the many outside boards she served on. By 8:30, Pringle was at her desk, on the phone, madly scribbling notes, making her way through 40 to 60 calls, while winding her way through 10 or so meetings daily. By 6 P.M. she was either scrambling out the door for a dinner with a client or ordering takeout and preparing for a late night at the office. Either way, she usually didn't roll up to her home much before 10 P.M. Despite Pringle's seemingly boundless energy, there was plenty of stress to deal with. Working with large accounts was often a tough, thankless job. "There was never any appreciation of the hard work we put in," Pringle confides. "It was always, 'What have you done for me this hour?'" But that was the price of success.

Soon the stress of doing it all began wearing on Pringle not only mentally but physically. The signs began slowly. There were the bouts with bronchitis, the chronic migraines, the wild 30-pound weight fluctuations, and a loss of memory. In the summer of 1989 she was sitting on the beach with her son when her heart rate dropped to 39 beats per minute. "I was sure I was going to die," she recalls. At the hospital the doctors found no heart disease, but cautioned Pringle to slow down her pace. She didn't. By the fall of 1989 Pringle was battling a chronic case of the shakes and had no energy. Three months later, she was paralyzed at her desk, unable to even call for help. Doctors told her she had chronic fatigue syndrome, a "stress-sensitive" disease with no know cause or cure.

After exhaustive testing, doctors concluded that the disease would require her to take an extended leave from her company. Pringle's husband and co-founder, Jim, managed the business while she took one full year off to recover.

Since then, Pringle has stepped back in to her company, trying to bring it back on track, and allowing others to be more involved in the decisions. But she is still not sure what the future will hold for her and her company, and for her as the CEO.

How can CEOs make this transition to strategic leader? It takes a strong commitment and willingness of the CEO to contribute to a solution rather than remain part of the problem. The first step is a psychological one. The owner must view the business as an entity separate from himself. This is a difficult separation for many entrepreneurs, given the enormous effort they put into launching the business. But just as a parent must let go of a child when he or she grows up, an owner must let go of the company once it has been given enough structure, control, and discipline.

MAKING THE TRANSITION TO STRATEGIC LEADER

Growing a business requires entrepreneurs to change their perception of their role as leader. The attitude changes from "I'm running a business" to "I'm building an organization." Those who view their jobs as "running a business" will never have the time or interest in the strategic activities and organizational development required for growth. One who is building an organization, however, is committed to and preparing the company for the long term.

The transition from owner-founder to strategic leader involves a conscious letting go of day-to-day business operations and entrusting a management team to run the functional aspects of the business. Granted, it is a long-term process learned over time. But the transition starts with a commitment by the leader to aspire to a new level of leadership.

The typical transition from owner-founder to strategic leader generally involves the following kinds of changes:

OWNER-FOUNDER	STRATEGIC LEADER
■ Does everything.	■ Builds team of competent managers.
■ Makes all decisions.	■ Builds the organization.
■ Knows every detail.	■ Charts long-term direction.
■ Involved in daily operations.	■ Creates and maintains culture and values.

(Table adapted from *Shaping the Entrepreneurial Company*, by David McKeran and Eric Flannigan, Management Books 2000, 1996.)

Are You the CEO or the General Manager?

Time for a reality check. Many business owners think that the CEO's job is to be a hands-on boss. However, the tactical and operational activities that many entrepreneurs define as their jobs are really more accurately descriptive of a general manager rather than CEO. If you spend most of your time baby-sitting employees, putting out fires, solving every problem, signing every purchase order, then you are not acting like the CEO. That would be more descriptive of a chief operating officer, general manager, or office manager. And that person will never have the time or vision to see emerging opportunities. If you want a growth company, view the CEO role as building the organization rather than running the business. There's a big difference between the two.

You are too involved in the business if any of the following apply:

■ You are the key person to manage day-to-day operations.

■ You make all business decisions.

■ You can't go on vacation for more than a three-day weekend.

■ You think and behave like a small-business owner.

That last point is to help you view yourself professionally. Do you see yourself as a small-business owner, or do you see yourself as leader of a multi-million-dollar growth organization? The business may grow, but leave the owner-entrepreneur in the dust. Many entrepreneurs grow their business to a sizable enterprise, but behave like they are running a mom-and-pop shop. The CEO of a $10 million firm should be thinking, "What would it be like if I were running a fifty-million-dollar organization? How would I feel, behave, and act?" As a company grows up, so must you.

Although it is a difficult challenge for some, it is the responsibility of the CEO to figure out how to both control operations *and* be a strategic leader. With the establishment of financial controls, performance metrics, and a capable management team, a good leader can manage the business operations without focusing all his time and attention there. To deal with this issue, some owners hire a second in command. Others reorganize existing management and staff. All company builders must at some point work themselves out of their own business operations. That is the foundation for healthy growth.

Learning to Delegate

The most effective management tool for facilitating the transition to Strategic Leadership is delegation. The longer owners maintain control, the longer it takes for other managers and employees to learn to make good decisions. The CEO must establish controls and systems with clear lines of authority and accountability, which will allow for delegation to take place effectively, and then build decision-making skills and responsibility among employees. Owners must allow employees to make decisions, and even to make mistakes.

Waiting too long to delegate can have dire consequences. Hedy Holmes, CEO of Hedy Holmes Staffing, thought she could do it all— make 10 sales calls a day, manage the sales reps, and run the company. But her health and profits took a hit. "The cost of sales was going up because no one was paying attention to the margins," she confides. When she finally brought on a sales manager, she says, "it was out of frenzy"—and it was a mistake. "I didn't take the time to make sure this person had business values complementary to mine. And I didn't do my usual due diligence—like asking for commission reports." The new sales manager lasted all of three months. It took Holmes many more months of networking and interviewing to find the right replacement.

Without delegation a business is entirely dependent on one or two individuals, with the business owner or a key manager as the hub of the business universe. That is not a healthy situation for a business to be in. For a company to grow, the business must be independent of any of the individuals it comprises. This level of independence improves the business operations, and increases its value.

Successful delegation involves the following:

1. Setting up the structures, standards, and procedures to guide behavior and expectations for decision-making. It is important to establish structures by organizing around functions and tasks, not around people. In the early growth stages, owners often find it easiest to use current employees for new projects or tasks as they emerge. But at some point this patchwork of people and jobs must be reevaluated: People must be assigned to tasks on the basis of their *competence* rather than on the basis of their *availability*. Then give employees and managers the tools, resources, support, authority, and accountability to make good decisions and run their departments effectively.

When John Sobeck started his Wilkes-Barre, Pennsylvania, company, in 1983, he worked 80 hours a week. But Sobeck had a vision: By age 55, he'd be his own man. Today, at 54, he works about 20 hours weekly at his $2 million fire and water damage restoration business, First General Services of Northeastern Pennsylvania.

For Sobeck, the years of preparation paid off. Early on, he wrote up policies and procedures so that new workers can learn their jobs quickly. He customized a computer program that holds all employees accountable, by keeping tabs on their activity. "The business could pretty much run by itself," boasts Sobeck, who annually invests from $20,000 to $30,000 in computer software and equipment that track the business's pulse.

The business is still growing: He and some partners opened a new field office last year. Meanwhile, he continues to spend his summers fishing in North Carolina. And when he's in town? He hits the links by 2 P.M.

Ken Hendricks, the CEO of ABC Supply Co., in Beloit, Wisconsin, also shows how setting up structures and procedures can work. He took his company from $183 million in revenue and 600 employees in 1986 to $950 million in revenue and 2,300 employees twelve years later. ABC Supply is a national chain of wholesale construction supply outlets that has landed on the *Inc.* 500 list three times since 1986. Hendricks installed systems that allow his managers to think and act as he would. He spends his time training his managers to think like owners. He gives them the financial and psychological rewards they need to run their individual stores. He has hired trainers from Domino's Pizza and Marriott International. Ken hosts an annual awards banquet to honor the top performers. He also provides managers with monthly financial statements for their stores, and teaches them how to interpret the numbers. At the end of the year, Ken distributes 25 percent of the company's pretax profits to employees according to the profitability of the individual stores. This structure allows Ken to focus on what he does best: finding ways to grow the business, rather than being bogged down in micromanaging the stores.

2. Creating appropriate measurements and controls that become the criteria by which to manage the business and to evaluate performance. "Delegation without information is suicide." says Kenneth Iverson, chairman of $3.6 billion Nucor, steel manufacturer headquartered in Charlotte, North Carolina. He explains how the success of his company comes down to delegation and controls. He says. "Every week all our divisions send headquarters a few key numbers that, taken together, give us a snapshot of their basic operations from beginning to end: quotes (bids), orders, production, backlog, inventory, shipments. Those numbers for all of Nucor's divisions are printed out on one eight-and-a-half-by-eleven-inch sheet of paper.

"A second weekly report, about four pages long, compares the current week's numbers with those of the preceding week, charts each division's numbers over a period of thirteen weeks, and compares the current quarter with the corresponding thirteen weeks of the preceding year. That enables us to look at trends. And since the reports are compiled by a computer, those comparisons are very easy to generate."

Nucor managers rely on about five pages of data to keep abreast of the weekly operations of 20 divisions across a multi-billion-dollar corporation. "I review the weekly reports every Wednesday morning over coffee," says Iverson. "If the numbers for a particular division look out of whack, we know we need more information."

The key, according to Iverson, is to identify the information that is truly useful, and then to concentrate on that information. "I'd suggest that you focus on information that tells you what you need to know under ordinary circumstances; that will give you an early warning when something extraordinary is going on," he advises. If your company experiences a precipitous drop in orders, for example, you want to know immediately, so you can find out why and figure out what to do about it.

3. Having the right people in the right positions with the capability to handle their jobs effectively. If any of these steps are missing, delegation can become an ongoing problem. The CEO then must continually step in to fix things and do it the *right* way. Successful growth companies pass on a decision-making framework to employees that replicates the CEO's quality of decision-making in concrete ways. The managers and employees are given the tools they need to make the best decisions rather than just take orders from the CEO. Appropriate structures and guidelines for decision-making also provide a common language for analyzing bad decisions or mistakes and figuring out what went wrong.

STRATEGIC LEADERSHIP ASSESSMENT

The following test can help you assess how well you are making the transition from entrepreneur-founder to strategic leader. If you want to get a more objective view, have some of your employees and managers take the test to see how they view your leadership. Have them take the test anonymously and return it to you via a third party, or by mail or by dropping it in a designated box. Compile the results and watch for any common themes in the responses. Invariably you will get some diversity in responses because all employees or managers experience their relationship with the CEO uniquely, depending on their particular role or function. But where there are similar responses, chances are that they reflect the truth of the situation.

Answer the following questions true or false.

1. Authority and responsibility are vague. It is unclear who really has it, aside from the CEO.   True___ False___

2. There is a lack of trust and respect for managers when it comes to allowing them to manage their areas.   True___ False___

3. There is a lack of business discipline throughout the organization.   True___ False___

4. The business is run according to the owner's intuition rather than a plan.   True___ False___

5. There are very few metrics for monitoring business performance.   True___ False___

6. The company cannot operate without the owner's presence and involvement.   True___ False___

7. Most decisions are still made by or approved by the owner, despite a management team's being in place.
True___ False___

8. Priorities are always changing.   True___ False___

9. The CEO views himself more as a sales, technical, or operations expert rather than as a leader.   True___ False___

10. The CEO always appears to be stressed and overwhelmed.
True___ False___

11. The CEO is overidentified with the business.
True___ False___

12. The CEO cannot go away on vacation for more than a three-day weekend.   True___ False___

13. There is a lack of camaraderie with or exposure to CEOs of other growth companies.   True___ False___

14. Employees are hungry for more leadership and overall direction.   True___ False___

Each of these is a symptom of a CEO who is not making the transition to strategic leader. If you recognize yourself in any of these questions, it is time to evaluate the future effectiveness of your role as CEO.

THE CEO'S JOB DESCRIPTION—EIGHT CRITICAL AREAS OF RESPONSIBILITY

What exactly does it mean to be a strategic leader of a growth company? He or she must engage in certain high-leverage activities that represent the highest and best use of their time and energy.

For example, John Huston, CEO of Advanced Circuits Inc. in Denver, has identified the issues that have a high impact on his business, and he devotes his limited time to those. He meets with important outsiders like bankers. He stays close to the company financials and reviews critical numbers each day he's at work. He meets with key managers and salespeople four mornings a week.

Like Huston, Robin Bradford, owner of Bradford Staff, in San Francisco, has thought about what duties really matter to her company. Recently, she and the top managers at her $12 million staffing business wrote down both the essence of their jobs and all their responsibilities. The results were surprising. Bradford discovered she was wasting time writing marketing literature and making sales calls—tasks that other employees could do. Delegating those duties freed her up to focus on the big-picture planning that is essential to her job. She also can devote one day a week to her outside interests, painting and art.

The following Strategic Leadership Profile outlines the most critical functions of the CEO. To determine whether you are performing them, keep a list of your various activities for two weeks. Then, read this guide and compare the eight categories with your current activities. If you find yourself involved in jobs that do not correlate with the eight categories, ask yourself two questions:

1. Should someone else in my company be doing that job?

2. Should I hire someone else to do that job?

If the answer to either of those questions is yes, give other people the jobs that are preventing you from being a good CEO. Focus your time and energy on the eight areas that will have the most impact on building the organization.

Each area of responsibility connects directly to the other Growth Drivers (Market Intelligence, Clarity of Purpose, Strategic Planning, and Infrastructure). The strategic leader is at the core of a company's growth, responsible for implementing each of the Growth Drivers.

1. Defines the Company's Purpose for Being in Business.

The CEO's fundamental job is providing a focused purpose and meaning for the daily activity of the business. This concept is often overlooked or taken for granted. Employees want to find meaning in their work, beyond the scope of the tasks they carry out every day. How does the business improve the lives of the customer? How does it contribute to society in general? How does it contribute to the employees and the community? These are just some of the questions that need to be answered.

The CEO must articulate the company's core purpose, and then communicate it to employees. The core purpose should capture the entrepreneur's passion for and vision of the business. The message should be reinforced and repeated often to embed it in the company's culture. At the heart of the purpose should be a sincere concern for the customer.

Dennis Bakke and Roger Sant, cofounders of AES (Applied Energy Services) Corp., in Arlington, Virginia, started the business with the intent of creating one of the leading independent power producers in the world. But, as AES grew, Bakke and Sant became convinced that the company's principles, values, and philosophy were more important than the profits. Bakke says, "People are thinking, creative, capable of making decisions, and trustworthy. They're unique, fallible, and accountable, and they want to be part of a group that makes a contribution to society." Bakke and Sant are so intent on sticking to their principles, that when the company went public in 1991, the SEC required them to state in their prospectus that given the choice between profit and principle, the latter would rule. Bakke instills his philosophy as he visits company plants around the world, meeting with employees in groups of 10 to 100. "I'm not talking about what kind of gas burners they're going to install," he explains, "We're talking about philosophy. That's the nuts and bolts of the business as far as I'm concerned."

A clear purpose also keeps the company focused. As a company grows and reaches a certain level of success, many opportunities emerge. Some are appropriate for the business, some are not. Having a well-articulated purpose will ensure a clear strategic focus.

2. Defines the Company's Future Direction

How well do the managers and employees understand your company's future? The CEO's job is to convey a vision of the company's future that will inspire employees. The CEO must show how the company will someday achieve some great goal, and how employees can contribute to accomplishing it. *People want to be inspired.* They want to be part of something bigger than themselves. Inspiration doesn't come from punching a clock day in and day out.

Setting a clear and compelling direction will give management and employees a sense that they have a future with their job and with the company, and that they are an important part of making it happen. It will also build excitement about the company. Think back on the last time you as CEO brought your employees together and told them, "I want you to be a part of something big. I want you to know where I believe this company is going. I want you to know why we are driving so hard. See, this is my dream for us . . ." That, to a great extent, is what leadership is all about.

After the CEO articulates a future for the company he or she must communicate that message in many ways and as often as possible. A mission statement should be more than some sentences on a plaque hanging on a wall. It has to be instilled through speaking directly to employees: telling stories, painting a verbal picture, describing the future goal again and again. This will be discussed further in the next chapter.

3. Serves as Strategic Pioneer

Being a strategic pioneer means exploring unknown territory in search of future growth opportunities. The CEO must be the first one to step outside of the status quo by pushing into new markets, capitalizing on emerging trends, establishing high-leverage strategic alliances, and ensuring that the company is positioned to take advantage of emerging opportunities.

To accomplish this, the CEO must keep up with industry trends and expose himself to influential sources, such as industry gurus, think tanks, innovators, and progressive customers. This is a time-consuming role, and one of the reasons the business owner must avoid getting trapped in the day-to-day operations. Growth will come to those who make the time to put themselves at the forefront of their market. "Somebody in the company has to think about what this industry is going to look like in five years and get ahead of that," says Ken Hendricks, the CEO of ABC Supply Co. "I would describe myself as a visionary." Hendricks has set up his business so he can be a *full-time* visionary, so he can spend his time developing new concepts that will differentiate his company from his competitors in a commodity business.

4. Sets Corporate Strategies and Leads the Planning Process

The strategic leader oversees the Strategic Planning process. This involves making the final decisions on which strategies to commit to, as well as ensuring their successful execution.

As the company grows, the CEO must maintain the firm's strategic focus. Many opportunities will come along—to acquire new business or to merge with existing ones, to form alliances, to get into new markets, to find new customers, and to develop new products and services. Although innovation and new initiatives are a sign of health, these new directions must complement and support the company's core purpose. The success of a growing company hinges on a small number of solid strategies that the business is fully committed to, rather than a hodge-podge of strategies driven by chance and circumstance.

It is up to the CEO to maintain this focus. Sometimes that means controlling your own impulses to do another deal. It may mean establishing a board of directors to keep you on track and sound off on new ideas. On the other hand, it may be some of your managers or salespeople that must be kept focused.

The strategic planning process is the best way to keep the entire organization on track (see Chapter 6). The planning process keeps the company's focus on doing only what it is committed to doing, doing it well, and then following through. The CEO must take ultimate responsibility for initiating and executing the plan. Without commitment from the top, the plan can fizzle out. The CEO must establish a clear and specific set of metrics that allows employees and managers to monitor and evaluate performance in each area of the plan.

5. Establishes Communication Channels Throughout the Organization

As a company grows, communication can break down as a result of the increased numbers of employees, customers, and business transactions. This can cause mistakes, loss of quality, ineffective performance, decreased productivity, and morale problems. The CEO must ensure that structured communication mechanisms are in place throughout the company.

Communication from the CEO should start with the fundamental purpose and direction of the business. A business leader should frequently address the entire company on the state of business, strategies, and plans. Employees find this information vital and exciting, but it is often taken for granted by management.

The CEO must pay close attention to how information is channeled throughout the organization, and take the time to structure it appropriately. There are many communication tools available such as Lotus Notes and e-mail to help with this task. But communiqués must be designed according to what information needs to get out, when, and to whom. At minimum, there should be a regular meeting forum for managers (weekly, biweekly, or monthly) to review current issues and future plans. Each manager should do the same with his or her employees.

The CEO should also solicit feedback from employees on an ongoing basis to monitor needs and issues, and to determine how well the company is addressing them. Some companies conduct internal "climate" surveys once or twice a year to get anonymous feedback on a variety of issues. Some CEOs try to have breakfast or lunch with every employee at least once a year. Others create an employee advisory group.

6. Fosters Company Culture

Every company has a culture. This culture is girded by a system of rewards and punishments, dictated by a set of unwritten rules of acceptable or unacceptable behavior. For example, in one particular firm, its culture was expressed in a casual dress code and a relaxed policy toward family members accompanying employees to work. Babies, children and even dogs are seen in the halls and offices. Employees are rarely micromanaged. At the same time, this company's culture is extremely results-oriented. Standards for performance are high and every employee is keenly aware of them. Those who want to slack off are not welcome, and don't last.

Ken Iverson, chairman of Nucor, says that the company culture accounts for the $3.6 billion company's success: "Without a doubt, Nucor's culture is its most important source of competitive advantage, and it always will be." He explains: "The culture has to be consistent to be real. Consistency is the name of the game as far as I'm concerned. And consistency begins with really believing in the culture you hope to shape. Nucor is founded on principles so basic they sound corny. We believe in treating people the way we want to be treated. That's a fundamental building block of our company. It sounds simplistic, but it works."

The CEO's behavior and language are the driving forces behind a corporate culture. Never underestimate their power. Everything you say and everything you do sends signals as to what is important within the company. Pay close attention to what is being reinforced in the organization. What gets measured? What gets rewarded? Who gets punished or disciplined? Who gets public recognition? The CEO and management team are role models for the entire organization, ultimately mimicked by the employees. If the CEO is a penny-pincher, then so will the organization be. If the CEO wears a suit and tie every day of the week, so will the employees. If the CEO is a workaholic, then so will the organization be. The management team must be aware of these tendencies and manage those standards.

7. Leads the Management Team

The CEO must develop a management team with the talent and depth to achieve growth. Once the team is established, the CEO must maximize the contribution from these managers. Many successful business leaders attribute their success to surrounding themselves with people smarter than they are. The CEO must spend time carefully selecting and then grooming the management team to grow the company.

Equally important as selecting the right individual players is the teamwork and synergy that should be nurtured at the management level. Managers should trust and respect one another. The CEO should ensure that management operates as a team—a unified front moving toward the same destination. Bickering, backbiting, power struggles or independent agendas only hurt the company. The CEO should confront those kinds of issues and resolve them.

As the CEO leads the Strategic Planning process, he needs to receive input from the management team when developing strategies and tactics. In the end, the managers implement these strategies and the planning process builds cross-functional connections between the different departments.

8. Pursues Personal and Professional Growth

As I've said earlier, if a company is to grow the CEO must grow both personally and professionally. If an entrepreneur is immersed in his business, he becomes isolated and insulated from the outside world. He will inevitably lose touch with his own weaknesses and limitations and be less effective as a leader.

It is the CEO's responsibility to pursue his own ongoing education in improving his leadership skills. The title of CEO or president does not automatically endow that person with a depth of wisdom, knowledge, and skills required for growing a company. Many CEOs and business owners never give a second thought to their own professional development, even though it must be proactively pursued. It can be achieved through attending conferences, seminars, university programs, peer groups, individual business coaches, or establishing mentor relationships. If you are never challenged, never think outside of your own four walls, never get exposed to other CEOs who have already been through what you are now experiencing, you will constrain your business's growth potential.

Along with personal and professional growth, it is equally important for the strategic leader to establish a sense of balance in life outside of the business. I recently attended a conference of CEOs where a keynote speaker recounted the story of building his business from scratch to a multi-billion dollar enterprise within a span of 15 years. From his presentation, it was clear that he had sacrificed much of his personal life for this achievement. At the end of the session, during Q&A, someone asked him how his business had affected his family. The speaker confessed that it caused a divorce and briefly alluded to the unpleasant nature of that event.

Although this situation is nothing new in the world of business and entrepreneurship, I was surprised by the reaction of the conference participants. Many of the CEOs at this conference were appalled by the blatant glorification of building a business at the expense of a family, and were adamantly opposed to this happening in their lives. I had individual discussions with several CEOs who essentially were saying, "I will never build this business to replace my family." The backlash response was surprising.

As a person's life is increasingly balanced, so will his or her fulfillment and effectiveness as a person. That balance for the CEO involves personal growth, professional growth, and nurturing relationships with loved ones. It is so easy for each of us to get caught up in the flow of work, the excitement of building a business, and focus on nothing else.

But how many executives will on their deathbed be heard saying, "I wish I'd spent more time at the office . . . "?

Most people, when they reach the end of their lives, will evaluate their time spent according to an internal compass that truly puts life in perspective, seeking satisfaction from a balance between making productive contributions to society and having the experience of love. Although this is a business book, I bring up this subject because we all have seen families destroyed in the wake of an entrepreneur's passion for the business and the exclusion of the family.

The negative legacy of a family torn apart will have an impact on generations to come that will last long beyond the life of a business. I simply pose the question: When is it worth it? There is a season for everything, and there may very well be a period during the early stage of start-up and early growth that demands extraordinary time, energy, and focus from the entrepreneur. But one cannot fully develop as a person with a focus skewed toward only one aspect of life. People will simply be more productive and effective when they are leading a balanced life, and that it is especially true for a business leader.

CHAPTER 5

Clarity of Purpose

THE MOST SUCCESSFUL COMPANIES REMAIN GROUNDED through the turbulent transitions of growth because they have a very clear reason for being in business, and a sense of destiny about fulfilling their purpose. This purpose provides an invisible pull on employees to contribute to something bigger than themselves, to create meaning in the work they do, and to find a sense of community among their coworkers. A company's core purpose also becomes the guiding hand for keeping focused on what it does best, and upholding standards of corporate performance.

Clarity of Purpose answers the question "Who are we, as a company?" It provides a context for work aside from the tangible inputs and outputs of the business, and gets at the heart and soul of the company. It addresses the company's unique significance, and how it will make an impact in the world. It goes beyond the material aspects of delivering the product/service to customers, and addresses *the meaning the business has in people's lives*—the employees', the customers', the life of the world at large. How does the business improve the customer's life? How does the company make the world a better place to live? How does the company deliver value to customers in a way that no one else in the world could do? How does the organization impact the community and the individual employees who work there, and their families?

As a company moves through the various growth stages, a clear purpose provides a fixed point by which a sense of stability is maintained. Although open to fine-tuning, a company's core purpose is not likely to change much over time in spite of the inevitable transformations required in strategy, markets, products, or business practices. A clear purpose actually *helps* the company to change and adapt as it grows.

Many entrepreneurs make the mistake of thinking they have discovered a compelling corporate purpose by posting a sales figure. "We will be a $100 million company in five years and then go public" is a theme that resounds through the halls of many growing companies. Although there is nothing wrong with having such aggressive performance goals, quantifiable targets alone will not likely capture the employees' imagination and enthusiasm. The real draw comes from articulating what a company is growing toward, how it will look, feel, act, and behave at its best—and the impact it will have on society.

Some may view the notion of finding meaning and purpose in business as irrelevant, but the truth is that without a clear focus, a company will have difficulty getting commitment and contribution from employees to work toward any one particular goal or strategy. When a company's purpose and identity are vague, people are uncertain as to why they are working so hard, and get caught up in the here and now. This can be further exacerbated when there is a sense of ongoing firefighting, crisis management, and shifting priorities in the workplace. The result is that employees are working very hard but wonder where all the hard work will eventually take them, if anywhere at all. The ambiguity and sense of meaninglessness can lead to burnout, mediocrity, and employee turnover.

A computer systems integration consulting and training company in the Northeast demonstrates this scenario. There are three owners, each with a particular area of specialization: training, networking, and interactive media. Over a period of several years, each owner pursued his own area of expertise, resulting in a company with three distinct business units under one name. Sales revenue grew to an impressive $5 million—it appeared that their trinitarian approach to business worked well.

But then the growth hit a wall. With 50 people employed full time, the owners found themselves frantically chasing every new opportunity (whether it made sense for the business or not) just to keep afloat. However, each of the partners became increasingly territorial in wanting to see his own area succeed. Employees received differing sets of priori-

ties and tasks, depending on which owner they spoke with. Each partner
pushed employees to follow his particular agenda. The frantic pace and
sense of shifting priorities eventually wore out employees. "We really
want the company to succeed," stated one manager, "but we appear to
be running in circles—making the same mistakes over and over. We all
want the company to grow, but we don't know where we're growing."
Another says, "People would be committed if the direction were communicated." Time will soon run out for this company, as talented
employees are leaving in droves while the owners struggle to determine
what business they are in.

YOUR BUSINESS FULFILLS A NEED

What every company must remember, whether its business is video
rentals or microchips, a machine shop or telecommunications, is that it
will survive and thrive only because it is fulfilling a need in the lives of
employees and customers, and somehow is making the world a better
place to live.

I was once speaking to a group of CEOs on this topic, and a gen-
tleman participating in the seminar appeared to be bothered by the discussion. He finally piped up and spoke his mind. "This all sounds
great," he began, "but I just can't see how this concept would apply to
every business." He was obviously having trouble finding any real meaning for his own business. The rest of us were up for a challenge, so I
asked him to engage in a little exercise. "Choose the most mundane,
meaningless business you can imagine," I said, "and let's see if we as a
group can find any purpose for that business." He quickly decided on
his choice—a dry cleaner. "How can somebody working in a dry cleaner's possibly find any meaning in that kind of work?" he asked with a
satisfied smirk.

It happened that another CEO sitting in the back of the room had
grown up in a family dry-cleaning business. "I think I can help answer
this," he offered. He quickly rattled off the following: "A dry cleaners
takes care of a sizable investment people make in their clothes. It takes
care of garments that we are fond of and that may have been gifts. Dry
cleaners make customers look and feel good for all occasions. As a boy
working in the business, I learned a work ethic that has stayed with me
all my life. My parents were also very active in the community and very

innovative in maintaining the environmental standards." This small family dry-cleaning business had a strong purpose for existence. "Watching the family deal with the ups and downs of running its operations has given me a wonderful perspective of what key skills, characteristics, and values it takes to maintain and grow a business over time," he concluded.

Managers at Manco, a manufacturer of labels, weather stripping, and duct tape in Westlake, Ohio, remind employees of the impact the company's adhesive tape has on the world by circulating letters from appreciative customers. One of the favorite Manco events cited by Marcia Carlson, national account team leader, was the contest soliciting customers' most innovative uses for duct tape. There was the pet tortoise whose cracked shell was held together with tape. And the photo that came in of the prize-winning apple tree grafted with tape. And the postoperative patient who used duct tape to hold her bandages in place.

Thanks to a heavy emphasis on training and information sharing at monthly companywide meetings, Manco excels at keeping all employees up to speed on the status and flow of its products from producer to end user. Diane Walsh, product manager in Manco's home-office-products division, says people in her manufacturing area "take pride in making a store display because they know where it's going." Walsh herself can't resist the impulse to check Manco displays whenever she's in a hardware store.

Another company that emphasizes the importance and meaning of its product's role for the end user is Great Plains Software, in Fargo, North Dakota. Dave Gaboury, Great Plains's original programmer, spends most of his time writing software. Like the other employees, however, Gaboury is expected to spend some time with customers, whether by manning the customer-service phones, monitoring the online customer-suggestion database, attending trade shows, or sitting in on new-product training classes. "You know customers are out there, but seeing them makes it real," he says. "When you learn that one of our products lets a manager do payroll in two hours instead of two nights, that kind of stuff really hits you in the face."

Odwalla, a maker of fruit and vegetable juices in Davenport, California, goes to great lengths to educate employees about the nutritional value of its juices. It also taste-tests potential new products in-house, holds product-naming contests among employees, and allots each employee a pint of juice for every day worked (two pints a day for drivers). The upshot of that effort for a driver making a delivery, says former-driver-turned-company-accountant Cindy Burns: "It's nice to have a product you can believe in. And you aren't afraid when you are asked questions."

The delivery-truck drivers are the ones who have the most face-to-face interaction with customers. The company has 35 trucks on the road, and each driver receives customer feedback at every stop along the route. Talk to the drivers, and you'll be convinced that they are the most enthusiastic advocates of the product. Odwalla has also invested over a million dollars in technology, outfitting each truck with a hand-held computer to track inventory and do invoices on the spot.

Bobbie Jacobs, vice-president of marketing, says that the drivers are Odwalla's public-relations team. Alone Arena, a former driver and currently fleet manager, concurs. "My friends tease me, say I sound like a salesman." But, Arena says, when you make a delivery, "you really feel like the ice-cream man."

IT ALL COMES DOWN TO PEOPLE

One of the fundamental reasons why a shared core purpose among employees can have such a powerful influence in growing your company is this: Your company is made up of individual people. Therefore, it will behave more like a community than a machine. If a company as a whole is to have a clear sense of purpose, each person who works in the company must have a clear sense of purpose for the work he or she is doing, and an understanding of what they are contributing to. Especially in deadline-driven work environments, the tendency is for workers to get caught up in the demands of the day-to-day workplace, losing sight of what they are actually contributing to (i.e., the end product/service in the customers' hands).

Whole companies are only as strong as their weakest links. When there is a clear and compelling purpose, employees will invest meaning in the work they do, and have a reason to care about how they perform.

Black Diamond Equipment in Salt Lake City hires the enthusiastic users of its rock-climbing equipment, and then capitalizes on their passion. "We breathe it, live it, think about it constantly," says the human-resources vice-president Meredith Saarinen, "which makes the whole company a marketing and design resource. It kills complacency." The message the company gives to employees is twofold: (1) What we do here makes possible a sport so devotion-worthy that people build their lives around it. What work could be more important? And (2) you and your coworkers are our ideal customers, so satisfy one another and yourselves. "It's not that our employees *can* make suggestions," adds Saarinen. "In fact, they have the duty to make them."

A SENSE OF PURPOSE—WRITE IT DOWN!

The only way that all of the employees in your company can latch on to this sense of purpose is if it is articulated and communicated, so that everyone knows what it is. It must be clearly communicated to all employees, so that they will understand how their individual jobs are contributing.

Kirk Hankins, CEO of Winland Electronics, says that getting employees involved in articulating the company's core purpose was one of the most important steps in setting the platform for growth. Winland, a Minneapolis-based company that designs and manufactures electronic components, was growing fast. But Hankins wasn't sure that everyone in the company was pulling together. "We were just fumbling along," he says. Even though the company was growing, he felt that the company was somehow out of whack. He had never run an entrepreneurial venture before, and felt it was very different from his previous life where he had managed a large division of a corporate enterprise. The employees did not all seem to be pulling in the same direction. Hankins began to second-guess his leadership skills.

Then senior vice-president of operations Loren Krueger attended an *Inc.* conference called "Growing Your Manufacturing Company," where he gathered enough information to come back to Kirk with a prioritized game plan. "The first thing we need to do is write down what we want this company to stand for," Loren said, "and to make sure we are communicating that with everybody." Kirk and Loren had a strong set of values and ideologies for running the business, but as the company grew from two employees in 1984 to more than 50 in 1997, they never got around to talking about these "softer" concepts. Hankins and Winland immediately went about the task of defining what they referred to as their "mission, vision, and core ideologies." They asked employees to vote for five candidates who most represented the employees and who would write down their view of the mission, vision, and values of Winland Electronics. Then they consolidated everyone's responses and compared it to their own.

"It was remarkable how close they all were," Hankins says. "That was a very good sign to me, and it became a very important step for the company." They then put their consolidated version in writing, and it stands now as the platform by which the entire company operates. When new prospects or customers come to visit their site, Hankins says he can select any employee at random to give a tour to the new customer and explain what Winland Electronics is all about. "Our employees are a lot happier now," Kirk says. "They know what's going on in the company, and how they are contributing to our future. They feel like they belong, and it shows in their work. You can see it in the smiles on their faces." With an annual growth rate of almost 100 percent in gross revenue, and a fivefold increase in net profits just this past year, you can bet Hankins and Winland have smiles on their faces too.

YOUR PEOPLE WANT TO BE INSPIRED!

Remember the movie *Jerry McGuire*? The story is about a sports agent who becomes frustrated and unfulfilled because he believes his firm has forgotten what the business is all about. The firm was started on the fundamental value that the clients—*as people*—were the most important thing, but this idea had been overshadowed by the agency's relentless pursuit of lucrative deals. Jerry attempts to bring the firm back to its roots by writing a late-night "mission statement," which describes his view of what is really meaningful and important in the business, and then circulating it throughout the office. The firm responds by firing him, because it now appears that he has lost his competitive edge. The agency staff shun him, except for one woman, a single mother who can't afford to lose her job. She admires and respects what Jerry has done and decides that having some meaning in her work is more important than job security. She joins Jerry in starting his new competing venture. On more than one occasion, she says to him: "Jerry, people just want to be *inspired*." She knows that on some basic level, everyone wants and needs someone or something to inspire them, and Jerry's bold mission statement inspired her. That's the point of Clarity of Purpose. People just want to be inspired.

Our experience with *Inc.*'s Growth Strategy Consulting Group has revealed this theme again and again. When we talk with employees, the message is almost always the same: they want their work to have meaning, and to be a part of something bigger than the scope of their daily agendas. They want to feel that they are making a difference in their life, in the world, in their company. They want to know that their work means something to someone. They want to be inspired.

It is the enthusiasm and perseverance of *individual employees* that allows a company to perform in extraordinary ways. The emotional and intellectual commitment of employees to transcend mediocrity is driven by their desire to make a difference in the world. When a company has a clearly articulated purpose and direction, it is able to draw more effectively on the creative talent and energy of employees, because each person understands what they are contributing toward, and how their contribution will impact the future.

Tim Plaskett, a shipping supervisor at Giro Sport Design in Santa Cruz, California is a case in point. Plaskett, an avid cyclist, was attracted to Giro because he liked the product, bike helmets. His appreciation escalated, however, when he began dealing with incoming helmets from the crash-replacement program—an offer Giro makes to customers to replace damaged helmets for a nominal fee. They're often accompanied by letters from grateful cyclists, who describe how their Giro helmets saved their lives. "This really makes you understand what you're doing," says Plaskett. To encourage all employees to appreciate the importance of the product, the company posts and circulates the letters.

Monette Paparotti, a customer-service rep for Giro Sport Design, is another example. Although the company attracts its share of hard-core cyclists, Paparotti was not among them. "As far as I was concerned, if there was air in my tires, that was fine," she says. Giro offers each employee a helmet at a discount, a perk Paparotti took advantage of. By the end of her first year at Giro, after rubbing elbows with fellow employees who were former world-class athletes, and having designers seek her opinion ("Do you like this color? Would you wear this?")— Paparotti was a convert to the helmets and to mountain-bike racing. When she is out cycling, she finds herself hailing those wearing battered non-Giro helmets and telling them about Giro's guarantee to replace damaged helmets for a nominal fee. "Here I am, out on the trails doing PR work for Giro!" she says.

MAKING A DIFFERENCE

A clear purpose will guide and inspire a company by giving it a sense of identity that goes beyond its products and services, beyond pure profit-driven intentions. The purpose will serve both as an anchor and a yardstick. An anchor to keep the business grounded, focused and true to its identity, and a yardstick to measure and assess every new opportunity as it emerges, to make sure that it fits with the company's identity.

In the landmark book *Built to Last*, the authors Jim Collins and Jerry Porras sought to discover the qualities and characteristics that drive the long-term growth and success of top-performing companies like Hewlett Packard, Motorola, 3M, and Nike. Using numerous financial performance indicators, they tracked 18 of these "visionary" companies against 18 comparison companies over the last 50 years. The authors found that the visionary companies outperformed their nonvisionary counterparts by a factor of two, and outperformed the rest of the market by a factor of 12.

What made the visionary companies tick? Porras and Collins concluded that the high-performance companies had a unique sense of identity (values and standards for behavior instilled throughout the organization) and a clear sense of direction (a corporatewide aspiration to literally change the world for the better). These core values had more meaning for employees than just pushing for bottom-line results.

Like those visionary companies, the employees of Group Publishing are out to change the world. Group is a $20 million publisher of young people's curricula for Sunday School and church education. Its founder, Thom Schultz, started the business because he saw a need among churches where most saw no opportunity and simply accepted the fact that church is boring for children and teens. Schultz wanted to find a way to develop exciting, dynamic teaching materials that would take a 2,000-year-old religious doctrine and translate it into fun and interesting learning that kids would actually enjoy. Schultz also had genuine evangelical concerns at heart. He wanted to connect kids with the message of the church, so that they would grow up with a positive impression and remain committed Christians throughout their lives. To Schultz, the financial results of Group Publishing are really secondary. They are a means of funding the company's primary purpose, which is to "encourage Christian growth in children, youth, and adults." Every key manager and employee at this company shares Thom's passion for reaching young people through dynamic teaching materials. They are literally out to transform the concept of Sunday School as we know it, and in the process affect millions of lives by making a long-term impact on children's desire and interest in their faith.

It stands to reason that, for Group Publishing, the passion and enthusiasm of employees for the mission of the company is strongly correlated with their faith, and that their religious convictions translate quite nicely to Clarity of Purpose in the business situation. However, there is no shortage of companies that have equal amounts of passion, enthusiasm, and commitment to their products or services in the absence of an underlying social, religious, or political agenda.

Take, for instance, GTW Construction Co. in Houston, Texas. GTW provides construction, maintenance, and rehab services for apartment and condominium complexes. Clem Majerus, the president of GTW, set out, like most entrepreneurs, to take advantage of some opportunities he saw in the marketplace. But somewhere along the way, he homed in on a higher level of conviction for what he came to believe was his company's core purpose for being in the business. He realized that the majority of the construction industry had a reputation for being somewhat unprofessional when it came to customer relations. For example, most people don't expect much regarding the appearance and conduct of construction workers. We've all seen or worked with construction crews who use foul language, have a dirty appearance, and leave a mess behind when they're done. And then the projects are rarely completed on time, or on budget. And if a phone call must be made to the construction firm, the telephone etiquette is not quite up to par with L. L. Bean standards.

Majerus decided he was going to change all of that in his company by building an organization that would set new standards for performance in the construction industry. He wants to literally transform the industry, and he believes that the values and behaviors of his company will be the site of that transformation. All of the actions, policies, and behaviors of GTW now reflect that goal. And the managers and staff of this company are just as enthusiastic and passionate to achieve that lofty goal as the managers of Group Publishing, the company with the underlying religious objectives. GTW has a clear purpose for its existence.

THE IMPORTANCE OF PASSION

Passion and emotion are essential to crafting a company's purpose. If the company's purpose doesn't elicit some kind of enthusiasm or excitement in those who hear it, it is probably destined to fizzle out. The company's purpose must connect with people at a gut level—in a way that conveys a sense of destiny. That is what inspires and motivates people to go the extra mile and to unleash their intellectual and creative energy for the company. Without this compelling sense of purpose, people will not feel responsibility or commitment. Their energy and enthusiasm will be diluted by a lack of corporate focus and direction.

Passion was the driving force behind Bob Metcalfe, the founder of 3Com in Santa Clara, California. "I view myself as participating in a technology crusade," he says. The evangelical fervor that propelled 3Com was a piece of computer hardware, a printed circuit board called an Ethernet adapter. The pace of progress in computing, according to Metcalfe, had been held back by the lack of compatibility between machines. He believed that this board was the key to the future progress of technology because it would create a standard for linking computers. "I was selling not the board, but the standard," Metcalfe said. He was out to change the history of the world through his technology.

Not that his zeal for the board alone would make it easy. He was up against a Silicon Valley competitor named Corvus which had already linked 100,000 computers through its proprietary network, Omninet, and IBM was working on its own standard, called Token Ring. But Metcalfe believed his standard was superior, and he even had a mathematical formula to prove it (this later became known as Metcalfe's Law). Founded in 1979, 3Com now has $1.5 billion in annual sales, while Corvus is out of business.

A genuine excitement for the business leads to a sense of discovery and destiny that will motivate and inspire people.

GETTING YOUR PEOPLE ON BOARD

Having a well-articulated core purpose allows you to both attract and retain people who are personally compatible with the company's intentions. Conversely, it also wards off those who are not compatible, who just don't get it. The purpose provides the company with a clearly defined set of standards and expectations for performance, and gives employees a sense of security, commitment, and enthusiasm about the future. The more compelling the purpose, the easier it will be to attract and retain the best and brightest talent available.

Clem Majerus decided that he would write a mission statement to capture his vision for what he wanted to do with GTW Construction. His desire was to create a company that would redefine the construction industry by setting new performance standards for professional service to customers. Although this is a common aspiration for many companies in a service-driven economy, it was quite original for a construction company. And Majerus wanted GTW to stand out in the market like a sore thumb. Once completed, he printed the mission statement on posterboard, blew it up, and brought it into the company lobby. Majerus gathered his employees together, pointed to the mission statement and explained to the employees his vision and why it was important to him and the company's future. Majerus emphasized that this was going to be the new operational standard for GTW from here on in. Then everyone went back to work.

Over the course of the next few days, several employees came to him privately complaining about two managers who were not living out that mission. These managers, who had a great deal of authority, had on several occasions blatantly defied the company's new mission statement and simply did not seem to care about treating customers as special. Majerus tore the mission statement off the wall. He then gathered his employees once again in the lobby and fervently explained why the posterboard had come down; it would not go up again until all employees behaved in a manner consistent with the manifesto. "The company was just not living up to it," Majerus explained. "I'm not going to have a big mission statement talking about customer service posted up for all to see when some of our key people aren't living it. It's just not right."

He then approached the two managers individually and gave them stern warnings. As the days went by, their behavior did not change, and employees continued to complain. After another round of warnings and subsequent complaints, Majerus decided it was time to let them go. They were clearly not GTW material, and they were bringing the entire company down to a level of behavior that was now unacceptable.

Majerus began to recruit for two new managers. This time, the mission statement itself became the standard by which he could gauge the candidates, because it represented the core of what the company was all about. Eventually he hired two new managers who completely bought into Majerus's mission and who saw GTW as an exciting and unique company that was going to change the industry. They wanted to be part of that. GTW's sales have tripled in the two years since. The management team is now an extremely dedicated, enthusiastic, and high-performance group. GTW's mission statement is the yardstick by which all corporate behavior is measured.

With a clear sense of purpose, you will be able to attract, motivate, and retain the caliber of people who are most willing to contribute to your company's future—especially if they feel that they are an important part of the success story.

Michael May is CEO of Empower Training & Consultants, a fast-growing technology training and consulting firm in Kansas City, Missouri. May knows that the future growth of his company comes down to one thing, employee talent, and he spends a great deal of time and energy on creating an environment that will draw and retain the best and brightest. May's motto: to be successful, business should first and foremost be fun. In the process of building that kind of company, he has found that his people want to help him perpetuate it. It's an upward spiral. "We've got the whole organization thinking and acting this way as a group," he explains. Everyone in the company can recite Empower's concise mission statement: "To become number one or number three in all markets we serve and to make this company fun, fast and fulfilling." (Number two is not included because May believes you should never settle for second best, and you need a place to sit when you're getting ready to go after number one.)

May wants his people to help him build "a billion-dollar valuation and a billion-dollar company—an ongoing, living entity that can't be stopped." The desire to build this unity of purpose among employees has translated into some fairly innovative and downright kooky rituals. For example, in the classroom training, Empower associates toss candy to the first person who works up the nerve to ask a question. And fresh-baked cookies get whipped up in Empower's kitchen and passed out during afternoon breaks. The most odd ritual of all, however, is the "Sparkle Fairy," who appears every other Tuesday at Empower's regular companywide meeting and sprinkles sparkle powder on new associates (to "sparkle" them) while reciting a poem:

This sparkle powder I give you today
Will empower you in a special way!
We hope you will always keep this in mind,
To make Empower one of a kind.

This eccentric initiation rite was dreamed up not by May, but by one of his first employees, Susan Burden. The "Sparkle Fairy" tradition keeps Empower employees true to the company's purpose, and captures in a word the kind of person the organization wants to recruit and keep.

AN EXERCISE: WHAT'S YOUR STORY?

In recent years, social scientists have come to appreciate what political, religious, and military figures have long known; that stories (narratives, myths, or fables) constitute a uniquely powerful currency in human relationships. . . . And I suggest, further, that it is stories . . . of identity—narratives that help individuals think about and feel who they are, where they come from, and where they are headed—that constitute the single most powerful weapon in the leader's . . . arsenal.

This quote is from *Leading Minds: An Anatomy of Leadership* (Basic Books, 1996), by Howard Gardner, professor of education at Harvard University.

Inc. magazine is filled with company stories. Anyone who has built a business from nothing to a successful enterprise has a great story to explain how it happened (if you have any doubts about this, just ask two or three business owners to tell the story of their business, and listen to their response). Along the way, there have probably been some definitive experiences that pushed the company to perform some extraordinary feat. Perhaps it was a crisis that caused people to rally together, or maybe it was an opportunity that required great risk and commitment, yet your people pulled it off. Or maybe one of your customers was extremely impressed with your company's product or service because you delivered above and beyond their expectations and saved the day for them.

Through these stories you can tap into your company's greater purpose and meaning, and get to the heart of what's really important—how the company is making a difference with customers, employees, or the community. Your company's story can also serve as the competitive tool that helps your employees define their sense of self, place, and direction within the company.

Take a few minutes to think about some of the greatest achievements in the history of your company. When did the company pull off some remarkable feat? What are your employees' most memorable experiences? When was the last time a customer simply raved about your product or services, or the way your company handled a certain event? Get together with some employees who have a longtime history with the company and reminisce for a while to stimulate your thinking. Then write down the stories that are most symbolic, or most represent what the company is all about.

Choose a story that stands out in your company's history and focus on the following questions:

1. What does this particular story say about your company?

2. What were some of the specific actions, behaviors and attitudes that were displayed by the company as a whole or by the employees involved?

3. What elements of this story are transferable to other situations (i.e., things that will stand the test of time, not tied in to a particular product or service)?

4. What lessons from this story are most important and valuable for the company?

5. Why are they important to the company?

6. What would you say is the moral to this story?

A CLEAR PURPOSE KEEPS THE COMPANY FOCUSED

As a company grows, it's easy for it to let itself be driven by opportunities that emerge rather than define the opportunities that it wants to create. Companies that are very "entrepreneurial" in nature are especially prone to jumping on every new idea that comes along. To make matters worse, sometimes individual managers or division leaders will start pursuing their own "once-in-a-lifetime" business deals. Before long, the company is fragmented, unfocused, and unprofitable—spreading its resources thinly among too many different kinds of businesses—and everyone forgets what business the company is *really* in.

When a company is in the early growth stage (Stage 1), seizing opportunities is fine because this is what drives the company from a start-up to an established entity. But the transition from entrepreneurial upstart to professionally managed firm is, to a great degree, dictated by the company's ability to get focused.

Steven Marks and Harvey Nelson got off to a great start when they opened Main Street Muffins in 1987. After renovating a condemned building in downtown Akron, 3,000 people came through the doors on the first day the retail bakery opened. As the year unfolded, the menu was expanded and Main Street Muffins evolved into a popular breakfast and lunch spot. Then, in 1988, a local restaurateur called to see if Marks and Nelson would sell him their muffin batter so that he could bake muffins to sell in his restaurant.

They jumped into the frozen-muffin-batter business with both feet, having no idea where it might lead. They purchased buckets and additional equipment, developed systems, and began picking up more customers. Soon they opened another store, and the batter business was bringing in 30 percent of total revenues. But as it grew, the business started having problems with cash flow, employee morale, and quality. By mid-1989, both the retail stores and batter business began a nosedive toward bankruptcy.

The partners had to make some tough decisions. "Harvey and I knew that instead of doing two things subpar, we needed to do one thing exceptionally well," Marks says. "We reasoned that to be successful (actually, to stay alive) we had to be focused. We had to devote our energies to that part of the business that had the best chance for success and that used our talents most efficiently. We believed that both the retail and the wholesale sides of the company needed full-time attention to make them profitable."

After a lot of wrenching discussions, they decided to sell the marginally unprofitable retail stores, but retain licensing agreements. The next thing the partners did was to write a mission statement that would remind them of their renewed focus, which was to "profitably improve an organization that overwhelms the food industry with its devotion to high-quality products and services." The most pressing issue at hand was dealing with the cash-flow and money-management issues. Within three months they became profitable again, and have been so ever since.

"Occasionally, my partner or I or one of our employees brings up an interesting idea for the company to explore." Marks says. But unlike in their early days they measure those ideas against their focus criteria: Is the idea consistent with our mission statement? Will it dilute our current efforts? How will it affect our operations?

Today Main Street Muffins has less than 2 percent of the U.S. muffin-batter market, but Marks and Nelson believe they can potentially get 8 percent to 10 percent or even more of the market. "Why would we want to dilute that effort by going off on a tangent?" Marks reasons. "If our sales slow down, then we may have to explore other opportunities. But for now we plan on being focused on being focused." Main Street Muffins' efforts to focus have paid off. Its sales revenue have increased at an average of 100 percent a year since 1990, putting it on the *Inc.* 500 list twice.

Clarity of Purpose ensures that the company will remain strategically focused on the few things that it does best and is committed to. Without this laser-sharp clarity, the actions of a company can dissolve into nothing more than an incompatible list of projects that are not taking the company in any particular direction or, worse yet, compete with each other.

WHAT BUSINESS ARE YOU REALLY IN?

At the heart of every company's purpose is a simple and compelling truth that can be communicated easily and that others can quickly connect with. If your company's purpose is clearly articulated and focused, it will reach out and grab people without requiring a half-day seminar to explain it. One of the best examples from recent history is John F. Kennedy's famous speech regarding the space program in the early 1960s, when the United States was in a race with the Soviets to land a man on the moon. Kennedy said that Americans would "land a man on the moon, and return him safely to earth by the end of the decade." The idea of sending a man to the moon didn't require a committee of engineers to justify or to explain the scientific possibilities. It was exciting, and easily understood, and was something that the country could rally around.

SatCon Technology is a manufacturer of electromechanical products, based in Cambridge, Massachusetts. Its work is very complex and scientific, but the company chairman, David Eisenhaure has simplified SatCon's mission into a very succinct, accessible concept: "We bring a higher level of intelligence to machines." Eisenhaure believes in what he calls "the elevator story": "You have to be able to describe to the person standing next to you what your company does before he gets off at the next floor. It's got to be simple. If it's too complex, then something's wrong."

Some of the largest and most successful companies in the world have been able to fuel their growth and success by their ability to remain focused on who they are and what they do best. Walt Disney is in business to "make people happy." 3M's mission is to "solve unsolved problems innovatively." Hewlett Packard's core purpose is "to make technical contributions for the advancement and welfare of humanity." Wal-Mart's: "To give ordinary folk the chance to buy the same thing as rich people." These companies are highly complex, but their statements of what they stand for are clear and easy to understand. Their emphasis on purpose, shared throughout the organization, allows them to grow into new products and markets while remaining true to their unique strengths, skills, and talents.

The best mission statements tread the tightrope between the world of ideas and the world of reality. They do more than simply give a sense of what the company aspires to in the world; they also say exactly how it intends to do it. There's a good example in the employee guide at Seattle-based Starbucks Coffee Co., which states the company's mission as follows:

> To establish Starbucks as the premier purveyor of the finest coffee in the world while maintaining our uncompromising principles as we grow.

> The following five principles will help us measure the appropriateness of our decisions:

> ■ Provide a great work environment and treat each other with respect and dignity.

- Apply the highest standards of excellence to the purchasing, roasting, and fresh delivery of our coffee.

- Develop enthusiastically satisfied customers all of the time.

- Contribute positively to our communities and our environment.

- Recognize that profitability is essential to our future success.

For many entrepreneurs, as they grow their companies they see more and more opportunities to expand and develop. Customers begin to ask for things. The management team comes up with great ideas. A niche opportunity opens up in the marketplace. All of which, on the surface, may make perfect sense for the company. The opportunities are too good to ignore because the company has the capabilities and wherewithal to make it happen. But the danger in taking on more and more unrelated initiatives is that soon the business is fragmented, unfocused, and attempting to be all things to all people. There is a great deal of activity but not necessarily any true progress or movement being made in any particular direction. Although tempting for many deal-driven entrepreneurs, the fact is that a company cannot do too many things and do them all well.

Safety 1st is an example of a company that faced this danger. It was a hot growth company in 1994, after the Chestnut Hill, Massachusetts, firm had become well known for its "Baby on Board" signs for car windows, which became very popular in the 1980s. Sales had tripled in just two years, and the stock increased from $12 to $32.75. But the maker of child safety products grew out of control and started launching new items in markets it was not familiar with, including deadbolt locks and door peepholes. It jumped on every opportunity that came along. The new products proliferated faster than anyone could keep up with, eventually reaching a whopping 650 products. The lack of focus and direction caused more than just confusion and inertia. The company lost more than $30 million in the three years prior to 1997 and the stock took a nosedive to $5.38. What happened? As their quarterly report stated, "Product offerings had proliferated to an unmanageable quantity, including products outside of [the company's] core competency." Now, Michael Lerner, the founder, says, "We're focusing on our core strengths. I wish we had done this three or four years ago. We have learned a lot."

Safety 1st has taken huge inventory write-offs as it slashed its product line, and now sticks to what it knows best—child safety products.

It is important for a growth company to focus on the things that it chooses to do well. The issue is less what the company does than *what business it's in.* Making some clear determinations gives a company the benefit of knowing what opportunities it should focus on and, equally important, reveals the opportunities that it should *not* pursue.

Diamond Courier Service, based in Philadelphia, had grown to $3.5 million in sales in just four years, due to the fearless sales skills of founder Claudia Post. But it had grown in so many directions that it was no longer the one business that Post had started; it was more like six. As she pursued the simple idea of running a downtown bicycle-courier business Post had seen and gone after other opportunities. Now, besides bike messenger services, the company was into driver deliveries, truck deliveries, air freight services, a parts-distribution service—and even a legal service that served subpoenas and prepared court filings. Although all the business shared some common resources, each had its own line workers, manager, and administrative-support practices, as well as its own steady customers and unique pricing and billing practices. The question was never, What do we do best? but always, What else can we sell?

But serious cash-flow problems began to mount, and Post decided it was time to take a closer look at the business she had created. After several weeks of careful examination, Post decided to shut down the bicycle messenger service, air freight, and parts-distribution divisions, forfeiting $400,000 in sales. Today the offices of Diamond Courier Services are much quieter. The company is healthier and there's cash in the bank. That lost revenue has been replaced by more profitable business. The company is focused on what it does best and what it can make the most money at: the more profitable vehicle delivery service.

This question of what business to focus on is not often easy to pin down as a company grows and evolves, but it is at the heart of future growth and success. Andover Controls is an example of a company that had several identity crises before truly understanding its core purpose. The Andover, Massachusetts, company started in the solar-energy business in the seventies, but never got too far. They then moved into the production of climate-control devices for buildings. But once again, the business didn't make any significant progress, competing with over 350 other "me-too" companies in the same market.

Bob Klein, Andover's vice-president of sales, says that once the management team realized that they were competing at the same undifferentiated level as all of the other companies, they decided to identify themselves in a different way. The competition was selling through large electrical contractors, the cheapest and most direct route to the construction market. But that diluted the energy-management systems, making them nothing more than an add-on to a building's electrical system. Andover decided it would instead focus on being in the "comfort business." It began selling through distributors that specialized in temperature-control systems, which better integrated their products into the buildings. As a result, Andover began to take off.

Today Andover is still refining what it means to be in the comfort business. It is starting to introduce its products into environmentally "intelligent" buildings, where security, mechanics, electronics, and electricity are tightly integrated. That means that they are involved more with specialized distribution and strategic alliances with other vendors. Of the 350 building-controls manufacturers that were competing for business in the 1970s, Klein says, only about 40 are still in business. Andover Controls, with $60 million in sales, is now among the five largest.

Taking the time to uncover your company's true purpose will not only help you to keep focused as you grow, but will also serve to frame the work—what your employees do every day—in a more meaningful way.

Production Testing Services (PTS), a $15 million company in Houston, does oil-site testing for the major oil companies. It sends crews of people out to remote locations like Siberia and the Arctic for weeks at a time to test drilling sites prior to the clients' setting up the big rigs. When I asked, "What business are you in?" most of the managers and employees responded by describing the technical aspects of the services they provide: "We dig a hole"; "We measure the characteristics of the ground"; "We test the oil quality." However, one of the managers (interestingly, the CFO) answered the question by saying, "We make our customers more profitable and productive!" PTS makes it possible for the big oil companies to select the most lucrative area for their oil rig, which has an enormous impact on profitability. The CFO's understanding of the impact they have on customers is a much more meaningful and compelling reason to be in business than digging holes in the ground.

The point here is that what your company does, technically speaking, is much less important than who you are and what your company stands for.

THE BIGGER PICTURE: THINGS GO BETTER WITH FOCUS

When Mark Kaplan thinks back to his days as a brand manager at Coca-Cola Co., he most relishes the intense focus of his job. "I ate, slept, and breathed Sprite," says Kaplan, who also presumably drank the stuff. "I learned to shut out every element other than those I needed to have vision for Sprite." That vision was to "beat 7-Up over the head" and make Sprite the number one lemon-lime soft drink—a goal he had achieved by the time he and his colleague Bob Solomon decided to strike out on their own, seven years ago, to run their own company.

Kaplan and Solomon were accustomed to strategizing and competing on an enormous playing field where products did more than just find and serve a customer base; they were marketed with an almost missionary zeal, and a lofty vision reigned supreme. The two weren't willing to leave that towering sense of purpose behind. "We had been with a company that was more than just a business proposition," he says. "Coke was the master of its product category."

Little did they realize how hard that would be to replicate this lofty vision at a small enterprise, where the big picture often gets blurred in the struggle for hour-to-hour survival. And the company they chose to buy, a small Atlanta-based chain of ice-cream stores called Gorin's Homemade, wasn't an obvious vehicle for worldwide domination. Although the company was just barely breaking even, Kaplan and Solomon were captivated by its tremendous name recognition.

Through their own grassroots market research, they discovered that although 75 percent of their "man on the street" survey sample were aware of Gorin's, fewer than 10 percent had ever been to a Gorin's store. "And there was something that people loved about it, whether they had been there or not," notes Kaplan. "I was very used to that kind of positive imagery at Coke. It made me excited, and I knew what to do with it." When he had embraced image-based marketing with Sprite, portraying the brand's devotees as young, energetic, and upbeat—is there any other kind of consumer?—the drink's popularity soared. Gorin's, he calculated, just needed some fizz; it already had the kind of image that many companies spend years trying to create, but it wasn't selling the right products.

"What the corporation taught me to do was to look beyond the day-to-day details and figure out how a concept would fit into people's lives," says Kaplan. "I really enjoy taking a brand that has strong awareness and making sure that it's exactly what the customer wants at that place and at that time." And that's what he and Solomon did. Ice-cream parlors, they concluded, were quickly facing meltdown. At Gorin's, they would capitalize on consumers' growing discontent with McFood by expanding the chain's small line of high-quality sandwiches and positioning the chain to fill the gap between fast food and full-service restaurants. Homemade ice cream would still be part of the mix, although it would no longer be as central to the company, now renamed Gorin's Homemade Café & Grill.

With the patience for process that large corporations teach so well, Kaplan and Solomon spent seven years transforming Gorin's, growing the company from 12 to 39 franchisees and quadrupling sales to $10 million in 1997. Along the way, the two have survived surly landlords, broken freezers, a flooded factory, and franchisees who were more interested in following directions than in contributing ideas. But what keeps the partners going—and sane—is that they've held fast to their vision of making Gorin's the premier restaurant in its category. "The corporate world taught me to maintain that focus," says Kaplan, "and every time I've forgotten that, I've suffered."

MAKING IT REAL: TRANSLATING CORE PURPOSE INTO EVERYDAY BUSINESS BEHAVIOR

Now let's bring translating core purpose into real life. It's one thing to talk about vague ideals such as treating each other with respect at all times, or providing remarkable service to customers, or to make people happy. But it's quite another to live these ideals out on a day-to-day basis at your company . . . to make decisions that are true to those ideals . . . to ensure that employees are acting in a way that is aligned. For those companies that have successfully maintained their purpose, they have found that it doesn't just happen. Instead it's carefully designed. They have formed *specific practices* that employees understand as symbolizing and representing the core purpose. These practices serve to nurture and reinforce the purpose, ensuring that it doesn't get lost as the company grows and changes.

Jim Collins, in an article entitled "What Comes Next" (*Inc.*, October 1997), suggested that organizations insert "mechanisms" into their business practices that reinforce their core purpose and convert it into action. For instance, 3M has as its core purpose "to solve unsolved problems innovatively." With innovation so crucial to the heart of this company, how do they ensure that innovation remains central in spite of many other kinds of opportunities that may emerge where they have the skills or resources? About 40 years ago William McKnight, one of the founders of 3M, proposed that employees take 15 percent of their day, at any time, to explore new business ideas. That policy nurtures innovation. It's not just discussed a lot at 3M, it's a real part of the business activity. The CEO's role, according to Collins, becomes that of an architect who designs the mechanisms that reinforce and give life to the company's core purpose.

Amy Miller has no problems establishing these mechanisms at her company, Amy's Ice Cream. In fact, from the beginning she has designed the ice-cream store chain in Austin and Houston, Texas, with one key purpose in mind: to create a fun, entertaining experience for customers. On the surface you will see the more obvious zany and fun antics that keep customers coming back, like juggling the serving scoops, or wearing pajamas on sleep-over night, or offering free ice cream to anyone who will recite a poem or mimic a barnyard animal. Miller's desire to sell entertainment along with cones has given her a definitive competitive advantage in her market against the bigger players like Baskin-Robbins, and has resulted in about 20 percent growth per year.

But there is method to Miller's madness. Entertaining at ice-cream stores obviously requires a special kind of employee, and she gets the message out via the application process. Instead of formal application forms, she gives candidates a white paper bag with instructions to do anything they want with it, and to bring it back in a week. "An applicant who can produce something unusual from a white paper bag tends to be an amusing person who would fit in with our environment," Miller says.

Applicants have used the bags to create cartoons, board games, and works of art, among other things. Those paper bags serve as the mechanism to screen and reinforce the importance of creativity in new hires.

Empower Training, the company with the Sparkle Fairy, is also intent on making its core purpose and values concrete by translating those concepts into everyday words and actions. These tangible, though sometimes kooky, behaviors are the essence of the company's unique identity. Whether it's trekking all 22 associates to the Sierra Nevada to celebrate reaching a significant revenue target, or getting sprayed with a squirt gun at a company meeting, Michael May, the CEO of Empower Training, has worked hard at developing an organization that is "fun, fast, and fulfilling." A company will reveal its true purpose through both its grand rituals and its everyday habits. At Empower, even the desire to ban the word "employee" (only "associates"—people capable of independent, rational thought—are employed) is a negative reinforcement device. If anyone uses the word "employee," "boss," or "manager," the cost is $5 per word to the offender. The collected money goes to charity.

Childress Buick/Kia Co., a car dealership in Phoenix, bills itself as "the friendliest place in town." For years that slogan was more of a description of the friendly founder, George Ray Childress, who was just as concerned with helping people and being nice as he was with building profits. But it wasn't until his son Rusty took the reins in the late 1980s that the value of niceness was actually built into the guts of the business operation. Childress believes fervently that service excellence and quality are the fundamental business principles that will keep customers coming back (crucial in the auto dealer industry), and that the key is to make employees actually care about how that is executed in the business. Childress's primary tool? Communication—compulsive sharing of information throughout the company. He explains, "By maintaining open communication with customers and employees, not only will you learn exactly what the customer needs and expects, but employees' job satisfaction will increase as well, which will help perpetuate your department's high level of service quality."

The employees at Childress have developed myriad tools to make that real—e-mail, bulletin boards, hot lines, newsletters, questionnaires, town-hall meetings, teams, and focus groups. Each tool is simple, low-cost and low-tech. Each on its own is unremarkable. But taken together and woven with a culture that perpetuates the same stories and words, the tools are powerful and make the ideal of "the friendliest place in town" a reality for any customer or employee experience.

For example, at "take 5" meetings, five workers are selected at random and are asked how they would improve the company. *Dealer Direct* is the weekly e-mail newsletter received by every employee with a computer. Employees are polled on a regular basis by means of an Employee Satisfaction Index questionnaire. There is the Suggestion Connection, a database that gathers suggestions, which are then reviewed and acted on by a special team. There is even an anonymous defect hotline, which puts employees directly in touch with Rusty. All communication efforts at Childress are channeled through an employee-run team specifically designed to improve internal communication.

The results are astounding—and the employees know it. Childress's Customer Service Index, the industry standards for customer-service in dealerships, has been hovering above 95 percent for overall customer satisfaction for the past few years. Employees are unanimous in their claims that the company is a great place to work.

DISCUSSION QUESTIONS FOR CLARITY OF PURPOSE

How clear are you and your employees on the true purpose for your company?

The following exercise will guide you in uncovering the unique purpose and significance of your organization. For best results this should be a collaborative effort among the management team and all employees. The feedback, insights, and suggestions from all the people within an organization will lead to a much more colorful and substantial result than from an individual working alone. The following questions should be discussed at length to draw out and articulate your company's core purpose.

- What makes us different from competitors?
- What are we most proud of?
- What are our best talents and strengths?
- What does our company do that others would want to benchmark?
- How do we make a better life for our customers?

- Why do customers buy from us rather than from our competition?

- How do we create competitive advantages for our customers?

- What do we want our reputation to be like?

- How do we make the world a better place?

Encourage everyone's participation and take notes on the responses that emerge from each question. Once you have discussed each question thoroughly, review the notes and look for common themes that are apparent throughout. Use these themes as the foundation for articulating your company's core purpose.

EAVESDROPPING EXERCISE

Here's another exercise for honing your core purpose: Imagine that you are in a restaurant and you overhear the people at the next table talking about your company. What would you ideally want them to say about your company? How would they describe it? What kinds of experiences have they had with your company? What is its reputation in the marketplace? In the industry or trade? In the community? With the general public?

WRITING YOUR FUTURE STORY

An equally engaging "story" exercise can be spun not from the past, but from the future. Unraveling the past can help your company tap into its deeper purpose and meaning, whereas envisioning your company in the future can help ensure that you are progressing toward a clearly defined destination.

Taking the time to imagine and articulate the future forces you to become more visionary as a company and think about possibilities that should be acted on now.

Imagine that your company has been selected to appear as the featured cover story on *Inc.* magazine five years in the future. The assignment is to write the article, using the following questions as guidelines:

- What is your market position and market share?

- What is your product/service mix?

- Who are your customers?
- How did you grow?
- What kinds of challenges did you face and overcome?
- What geographic areas is the company operating in?
- What is it like to work for the company at this time?

Have each person involved in the exercise write his or her article independently; they then come together and share stories. It is a fun way to begin imagining your company's ideal future.

A GREAT EXAMPLE: GIRO SPORT DESIGN

Giro Sport Design is a company that articulated its core purpose in a way that is truly inspiring. Located in Soquet, California, Giro manufactures bike helmets. This statement, created several years ago, is being fulfilled today, when the company's helmets are considered to be the leaders in the industry.

MISSION AND VISION OF GIRO SPORT DESIGN

Giro exists to make a positive impact on society—to make people's lives better through innovative, high-quality products. . . .

The best riders in the world will be using our products in world-class competition. Winners of the Tour de France, the World Championships, and the Olympic Gold Medal will win while wearing Giro helmets. We will receive unsolicited phone calls and letters from customers who say, "Thank you for being in business; one of your helmets saved my life." Our employees will feel that this is the best place they've ever worked. When you ask people to name the top company in the cycling business, the vast majority will say Giro.

CHAPTER 6

Strategic Planning

HAVING A PLAN ISN'T THE SAME AS HAVING A CRYSTAL ball, but the most successful growth companies have made it through the critical humps because they have a planning process in place. In essence, they possess an orderly and disciplined approach to building their companies. Rather than experiencing the much-discussed chaos and frantic pandemonium associated with rapid growth, the companies that are serious about their planning process find their growth to be orderly and structured. Unfortunately, few aspiring growth companies ever get around to doing any disciplined planning. They think that they're too busy surviving through each day to take the time to plan, and most problem solving and strategizing is done on the fly. If this is the case, the future goals of the company will be buried under the mundane details of everyday tasks, and the company will be unlikely to progress toward growth.

Strategic Planning is the fundamental process by which a company determines specific action steps to achieve future goals. It is the map to guide your activities on the way to your destination by providing the specifics that need to be done when, by whom, and with what resources. Planning allows the company as a whole to focus on the right priorities and activities to accomplish the corporate goals, and is one of the key management activities that will allow a company to proactively manage its growth. This doesn't mean that moments of crisis or setbacks won't arise, but overall a company's successful growth can be very well thought out and well planned. And when it is carefully planned, the risk of failure is minimized.

Planning offers management an invaluable opportunity to step back from the day-to-day concerns of running a business and take stock of where they're going and where they've been. Companies that are experiencing rapid growth but don't concern themselves with planning eventually will either stagnate or, worse, will begin to lose control of cash flow, credit lines, customer service, and product quality.

STRATEGIC PLANNING WORKS WITH OTHER GROWTH DRIVERS

To get a handle on strategic planning consider it within the context of the previously discussed Growth Drivers: Market Intelligence, Strategic Leadership, and Clarity of Purpose.

Strategic Planning and Market Intelligence

Market Intelligence puts you in touch with the realities of the marketplace—the competitive environment, trends, and customer needs and wants—allowing you to ensure that business strategies and goals are in tune with the outside world. What if there are new advances in technology? What are competitors doing? What kinds of changes are customers going through? For many companies in the planning process, this kind of information is ignored. The finance department asks the salespeople how much they think they can sell, and then tells them whether that's enough. Planning is nothing more than budgets taken from previous years and revised for the upcoming year.

If Market Intelligence is weak, then the plan will be based on invalid information or internally driven data that does not jibe with the competitive realities of the outside world. This approach hides the company from the shifts and changes of the marketplace, so when the plan gets executed the market may not respond. Market Intelligence is a critical predecessor to Strategic Planning because it ensures that the entire management team understands the challenges that are being presented from the external environment.

Strategic Planning and Strategic Leadership

Without the support of a company's leader, plans will become nothing more than dust collectors rather than tools that actually mobilize the company. Strategic Leadership ensures that the organization has a capable CEO with the skills to pull people together and motivate them effectively to work together to follow a plan. If Strategic Leadership is weak, then the plan is destined to fizzle out for a variety of reasons: lack of follow-through and accountability; lack of effective decision-making among employees; low morale and motivation because of an overcontrolling entrepreneur.

Tony Rigato is an entrepreneur who discovered his leadership flaws in the course of the planning process. Rigato is CEO of MRM, a distributor of pneumatic industrial components in Novi, Michigan. Upon his first attempt at strategic planning with the management team, in 1991, he told each of his team members to be completely honest. So when the subject of MRM's weaknesses came up, Todd Brieschke, then the company's Toledo branch manager, noted that one of the company's biggest weaknesses was standing right before them: Tony Rigato himself. He had been "leading people by kicking them constantly," Brieschke said. The others agreed, and Rigato soon found himself filling two flip-chart pages with his own management flaws: "overrides managers' decisions," "doesn't respect peers and subordinates," and "inconsistent leadership." By the end of that first session, Rigato had a completely different attitude about his role as CEO. "That first session made me realize that I could have all the great ideas in the world, but if I didn't develop some leadership skills, it would all be in vain." Rigato knew that unless he transformed his own leadership style, he could do all the planning in the world and never meet his goal of growing from $4 million to $10 million in three years. His company would remain stuck where it was.

Strategic Planning and Clarity of Purpose

Clarity of Purpose provides the backdrop for evaluating your company's strategies and goals by establishing some overarching truths and standards to live by, allowing the company to know itself and to remain focused. If a company is going about its planning process but is not clear on its purpose and direction, it runs the risk of taking on initiatives and projects that are not necessarily in the best long-term interest of the business. Or, the big dream for the future just hangs out there, without any coordinated activity moving the company toward it. A vision for the future won't amount to much without a strategy and an organization to achieve it.

Planning, then, must be developed within the context of these three Growth Drivers. If any of them are missing, the planning will be ineffective, because planning in and of itself cannot mobilize a company to move from one level of growth to the next. The first three Growth Drivers provide the "big picture" for the company, and once that big picture is in place it becomes much easier to fill in the details. It's like doing a jigsaw puzzle—you throw all of the pieces of the puzzle out onto the table and begin by putting the border or frame in place. When the outside frame is done, it becomes easier to fill in the other pieces of the puzzle. The same is true in a business. The Growth Drivers provide the frame for the business. Once you understand the marketplace and your customers' future needs, and the appropriate leadership skills required to grow, and you have articulated your core purpose, you have developed the framework by which the details can be managed. You can now ask the important questions about exactly how the business will get from point A to point B. Should you be developing new products or services? Should you begin to pursue new or different types of customers? Should you be entering new geographic territories? Which new opportunities should you capitalize on? What kind of timetable will be followed?

PLANNING IS BASIC

Planning represents the very practical methodology for turning the dreams for your business into reality. Many entrepreneurs have grandiose, bold, and aggressive visions of their future, but just having dreams will not necessarily make it so. At some point you have to get out and do the work to make it happen. You can't think and visualize your way to effective growth. On the other hand, many companies are operationally excellent, but have very little vision for the future. These companies have their execution of operations honed down to a science, but have not spent any time planning where they want to be in the future.

One dynamic educational video production company in the Northeast demonstrated both extremes—a bold vision for the future and an extremely fine-tuned operation. The company had grown to $6 million and clearly had great potential for future growth. Its founder and CEO was truly passionate about the business, and had spent a great deal of time with his employees on fine-tuning the business operations. Using the latest techniques of Total Quality Management and Continuous Improvement, the operations were running at an extremely high level of efficiency with very few mistakes. Charts and graphs were up on the walls displaying the target indicators and goals for quality and production. Any maven of corporate standards would have been impressed by this company's attention to quality and detail.

The CEO also was a big thinker and had lofty aspirations for his company's future. Given the convergence of changes in both educational reform and the technology opening the way to distance learning, he was out to create an entirely new model for education, and he knew the opportunities would flourish. To capture the future vision, he had gone so far as to create an in-house company video telling the story of the company 10 years in the future. It was an imaginative and fun video, with props, special effects (it was, after all, a video production company), and clips of each of the managers playing the role of commentators documenting the story of the company's success. The company also had very carefully crafted mission and vision statements describing its purpose and intentions.

Even though the company had a high level of operational proficiency and a terrific vision for the future, the CEO and managers felt that something was missing. "I can't put my finger on it," says one manager, "but there is a morale problem here. Some folks are not grasping the vision—they don't *own* it." Another states: "I sometimes get caught up in the day-to-day activity and lose sight of the vision." The problem? There was a huge gap between the push toward the company's future vision and the pull of the day-to-day operations, and there was a great deal of tension between the two. The employees were driven by very high standards for operational performance, and there was also pressure to achieve the goals for the future vision. But nothing connected the current operation with the future goals. New markets had been identified as targets consistent with the vision, but the details about how these new markets would be attacked and with what resources remained very fuzzy. Management felt that there was far too much pressure on maintaining current operational standards, and they didn't have the time, resources, or clear priority to pursue some of the new ideas for growth. It was as if two completely distinct concepts existed within the company: the future vision, and the current operation. The result was an uneasy tension felt by management.

The solution was obvious: a strategic plan that connected the current activities with future goals. The company had never taken the time to develop a planning methodology, and as a result, it was running hard after both short-term and long-term goals without a management tool to pull them together. The management team now regularly conducts an off-site planning process to focus on the issues that will move them toward their goals while maintaining the operational standards that it has worked so hard for. The tension doesn't exist anymore because people have a clear path to follow.

Another company, Production Testing Services (PTS), in Houston, had a similar experience. PTS had a goal, set by the CEO, to grow from $10 million to $100 million in five years and then to go public. This is certainly an admirable and ambitious goal. But from discussions with the various members of the executive team, it was apparent that none of them actually *believed* it could happen. They each viewed that future goal as more the CEO's pipe dream than a real possibility. Why? Because once again, there was no *plan* to show how it was supposed to be played out. Therefore, it wasn't real, and in their minds growth was simply going to be the result of faith, hope, and good luck.

PLANNING IS A KEY MANAGEMENT DISCIPLINE FOR GROWTH

If you want your company to grow, planning is a critical management discipline that must be incorporated into the regular activities of the organization. Going through the mental exercise of putting a plan together and committing it to writing forces a company to think through the logic of its growth strategy in black and white. Sloppy logic, emotional decisions, and weak links all become exposed under the light of good planning. Many growth companies, however, ignore planning because they think it is too complicated, or because they don't have the time. Other CEOs use the excuse that they are not sure how to do it, or that "things change too fast."

But planning is as important to a business as, say, developing sound accounting practices. Without a plan, the business is likely to be operating from a reactive stance, taking its cues from the push and pull of the market, customers, or individual managers rather than from a predefined path. A business that does not plan is at the mercy of its environment to a much greater extent than one that proactively defines the environment it wants to operate in.

Planning is one of the key activities that helps a company evolve from a small, mom-and-pop shop to a professionally managed firm. As a company grows and becomes more complex, it becomes too difficult and complicated to be run out of the entrepreneur's head (remember "Management By ESP"?). With a greater number of employees, customers, transactions, physical sites, and decisions to be made, the need for communication and coordination increases greatly. A plan provides the mechanism to coordinate and focus the activities of the organization so that everyone is moving in the same direction. It ensures that the most important priorities are identified and that they are accomplished at the right time in order to move the company in the right direction.

Some would argue that the words "planning" and "entrepreneurial" don't even belong in the same paragraph. Shouldn't entrepreneurial companies be adaptable, flexible, and able to move quickly in a fast-paced, ever-changing marketplace? A start-up company in Stage 1 rarely has a serious business plan in place because it is continuously evolving and exploring opportunities as they emerge. These companies need the ability to turn on a dime rather than being tied down to some corporate dictate for every move it makes. But when that same company discovers its niche in the market and starts to expand, planning becomes more and more important.

The seat-of-the-pants management style that characterizes so many gun-slinging maverick entrepreneurs can only support a company's growth for so long. As a company expands, the number of customers, financial transactions, and employees increases dramatically. Before long things start slipping through the cracks. It becomes impossible to keep track of who's doing what, and which of those activities are making money. Smart companies utilize a planning process to focus their organizations on controlled growth, orderly operations, and predictability. Yes, the market environment will continue to change and shift, but having a plan in place coordinates the various complexities involved in managing a larger enterprise. The plan also provides a guide for questioning potential deviations in order to avoid reactionary decisions to short-term events.

David Harmon is the president and CEO of El Camino Resources in Woodland Hills, California, a fast-growing computer leasing and reselling company. He articulates the importance of planning to entrepreneurs: "When you're small, you can almost put your plan on the back of an envelope. Now it takes a whole three-inch binder." What changes as a company grows, he says, is that planning becomes even more critical—and more complicated and formal, since there are more variables to track. Today El Camino has more than 500 employees and $667 million in sales. However, with the rapid-pace changes inherent in the technology field, El Camino still has to remain flexible. A good plan allows entrepreneurial companies to remain flexible, yet within the context of a structured plan.

Albert Van Kirk, CEO of King's Medical Co. in Hudson, Ohio, attributes the company's success through the early stages of growth to planning. King's Medical owns and manages magnetic-resonance-imaging (MRI) equipment—million-dollar-plus machines used by hospitals, that produce X-ray-type images. With 32 sites in 14 states, King's Medical took on massive debt while growing some 400 percent between 1987 (when sales were $2.7 million) and 1992 (when sales were $14 million). During the same period, some companies in the industry went public and became better capitalized. Still, Van Kirk says King's Medical held its own, claiming 12 to 20 percent profit margins while two of its publicly traded rivals showed profits of less than 5 percent and another registered red ink. King's Medical, which has since doubled its 1992 sales, attributes its success to its planning process—specifically, the decision-making discipline and follow-through that it promotes.

Tony Rigato of MRM found that the planning process prompted him and his management team to rethink the company's relationship with some of the manufacturers whose products it distributed. In 1994 the planning team concluded that the company's relationship with its largest supplier no longer jibed with MRM's long-term strategy. Moreover, MRM was spending 70 percent of its resources on that supplier's product line, though it accounted for only 40 percent of MRM's revenues. Rigato was faced with a dilemma: Should he stick with his strategic plan, or with the supplier company that had been the mainstay of his business for 25 years?

Tony and the employees thought analytically about the decision, in accordance with the precepts of strategic planning. As he contemplated dropping MRM's biggest source of revenue, Rigato outlined a sales-replacement strategy and pledged that no one would be laid off. "I could show them through the strategic planning how the decision could be made and how we could survive," he says. "And that gave me the confidence to pull it off." In 1995, after more than two years of analysis and preparation, he did pull it off. Two years later, MRM's sales rebounded from $7 million to $13.5 million. The long-term results have also justified the decision: Rigato reports that since 1991, sales have more than tripled, profitability has increased substantially, and employee turnover has reached an all-time low. "None of what we've been able to accomplish would have been possible without Strategic Planning," he emphasizes.

OBSTACLES TO PLANNING

There is nothing mysterious, complicated, or revolutionary about planning. So why do so few companies engage in the planning process?

The first problem is always a lack of time. For those concerned about the issue of time, the truth is that they're right—there's never enough time unless you make it. The issue is really one of priorities rather than time: How important is it for you to achieve your growth goals? Where will your company be in five years if you don't change anything about the way you are doing business? How competitive will your company be if it is operating from a reactive rather than proactive mode? How effective will employees' performance be without a coordinated plan for corporate focus and priorities? How will decisions be made regarding allocation of resources? Planning the time for planning is the first step in the planning process! And the companies that utilize planning at some level will be more likely to increase their long-term effectiveness compared to those who don't. Management must recognize planning as a strategic priority and allocate to it the appropriate time and preparation in order to make it happen.

The second issue is an uncertainty regarding technique. "No one in the company has ever done strategic planning before, and we don't know how," is a common response to why there is a lack of planning. Often the management team will shy away from planning because they're unsure of the "right way" to do it. There is no magic formula or absolute standard for conducting a planning process. If you were to ask 10 planning experts, you would probably get 10 different methods, all variations on the same theme. The truth is that planning is not an exact science, and the technique is much less important than the process itself. It is far more important and beneficial to the company to take a stab at it and get management together to think and talk about the execution of corporate strategy rather than do nothing at all. Your plan will not be wrong because it fails to follow some special format. Some CEOs argue that by the time you have written a draft of the plan, you've gained 90 percent of the benefit from the process. The exercise of planning in and of itself is far more valuable than any particular process used.

At Frontier Cooperative Herbs, in Norway, Iowa, the management team has been writing annual strategic plans since the early 1980s. An *Inc.* 500 company founded in 1976 that distributes spices and other products to natural food retailers, it grew from $2 million in 1982 to more than $31 million in 1997. When CEO Rick Stewart looks back on some of those first plans, he admits that "there were a few plans in the early years that were really compost." That's okay, because Stewart contends that just the process of planning puts a company on the right track, because it gets the key staff members to agree on important goals. "It's more important to finish the plan than to do everything right," he says. "You can always get better at it next year." The first step in Frontier's annual planning process is, in fact, figuring out ways to improve on last year's planning process.

Planning is a learning process. One can get only so far through market analysis and internal discussions of the company's potential. Ultimately, you have to put ideas to the test, and learn by doing. Don't expect perfection with your first few attempts. It may take several years of going through the planning process with the management team before everyone starts feeling good about the finished product. As your company engages in the planning process as a regular management activity, it will get better and better with each attempt, because you will be teaching yourselves along the way.

MRM's Tony Rigato has held an annual off-site planning session each year for the past six years, and notes that each year the planning team took a more sophisticated approach. They started with a template-driven model based on a strategic planning seminar that Tony had attended, but as the management team conducted the process and observed the results of the plan year after year, they found new ways to fine-tune and improve the process.

PRACTICAL SUGGESTIONS

Guidance for Planning

There are three common sources you can turn to for planning assistance: professional facilitators, books, and seminars. See the Resources section in Chapter 8 for specific information on each type.

If you are gun-shy about jumping into a full-fledged planning process, try using a professional consultant or facilitator—someone who can facilitate the process, provide objectivity, keep the discussions focused, and provide a reality check for the ideas that emerge and their implications in execution. Many business owners find that using outside facilitators in the planning process is an invaluable resource. The best way to find a good facilitator is to network with other CEOs who have had positive experiences.

There are many professionals familiar with the planning process, some who make it the focus of their work. An outside facilitator can benefit the company in many ways. It can be useful to get an outside perspective on the challenges and issues that your people have been dealing with every day for years. Sometimes a fresh mind can bring obvious solutions and points of view to a home-grown management team by asking good, basic questions about what your assumptions are and why (questions that sometimes don't get asked internally). In the process, an outside facilitator can also provide an objective and nonemotional rationale while dealing with the tough issues that may be too close to home for certain members. And for those who just don't know how it is done, a professional facilitator can provide a ready-to-use template or process to guide the management team, keep the momentum going, and make sure that the process stays on track.

Other Planning Tools

These two culprits—lack of both time and technique—can paralyze a company from ever attempting planning for years and years. To help break this inertia, try these practical tools and tips.

Have an Off-Site Meeting

First, go away! Plan an off-site planning meeting with the management team. Effective planning cannot be conducted in the midst of the everyday work environment. Interruptions, telephone calls, and the "to do" list will be extremely distracting and will end up pulling people away from focusing on the project at hand. Most companies that are involved in planning spend two to three days off-site, away from the distractions of the office, in order to focus exclusively on the planning process.

Shefsky & Froelich Ltd. is a Chicago law firm that employs 57 lawyers, though back in the early eighties there were just 10 lawyers. Even back then, it wasn't easy to get them all together to focus on strategic planning. Like most partners in small enterprises, they would rather be taking client calls than taking the time to plan. So one weekend, Lloyd Shefsky recalls, about five partners gathered at a lakeside resort to talk about their long-term goals for the firm. They all brought tennis rackets, expecting to relax after their strategy session. Instead, the partners spent most of the weekend huddled around a small table in one of the rooms, hashing out key issues. By the end of the weekend, no tennis had been played—and though the lawyers had agreed on overall goals, they still hadn't decided how to reach them. The next weekend they reconvened at one partner's home and blocked out a strategy to achieve that growth. "We created what we today would call a business plan, but then it was very simply a format for accomplishing the goal," Shefsky says. Was it worth the trouble? Apparently. Shefsky says the firm is still following that original plan.

Get Managers Involved

It is extremely important to tap into the often hidden sources of ideas and innovation that exist within the management and key employees. Planning forces two-way communication to occur between management and the CEO. Small companies in particular need this dialogue, since many CEOs don't let the rest of the organization know why they're doing what they're doing. One of the payoffs of the planning process is that is allows managers to see how actions and everyday decisions fit into a broader picture. Another benefit is that involving a cross-section of managers in decisions helps to smooth the way from idea to implementation. Their input, feedback, and perspective will not only enhance the end result, but will help them each take ownership of the plan, and understand how the different divisions and departments are affected by the execution. The bottom line is that the managers are often the ones who ultimately implement much of the strategy at an operational level, so it is always a good idea to get them involved with the process.

Sixty-year-old Malley's Chocolates, in Cleveland, is typical of many privately held companies in that it has a few key decision-makers. But in 1993, when the president, Bill Malley and his wife, executive vice-president Adele Ryan Malley, resolved to develop a formal strategic plan for the family business, they found that planning was a good way to bring new voices into company decisions. All five of the third-generation family members who work for the company got involved. The result, says Adele Ryan Malley, is that the younger relatives are gaining a more complete understanding of the operations of the company, which has more than 200 employees. "It's giving the third generation some more opportunities to take a different look at the business," she says. "Now they understand more about the worries." The same principle applies in any company, even when family isn't involved. Creating a plan offers a great opportunity to delegate, hear opinions from employees, and groom talented young managers.

It may also be useful to involve other outside people in the process, such as other executives, bankers, lawyers, and accountants to ask probing questions. This allows you to ensure that all decisions are informed and relevant.

LAYING THE GROUNDWORK FOR THE PLANNING PROCESS

To begin the Strategic Planning process, start with a review of your core purpose and define your long-term goals and direction for the future. Remember that the strategic plan should be designed to *support* the core purpose and *achieve* the future direction.

I. Core Purpose

To start the planning process, the leadership team must first define in the clearest terms possible why you are in business. The first crucial question to be absolutely nailed down is: What is our core purpose?" The question of core purpose is addressed fully in Chapter 5, where there are exercises to assist a management team in defining the focus of the business.

At King's Medical, each board member and the CEO have to answer some of these basic questions prior to their Strategic Planning process, and write down their own conceptions of the company's purpose. One of the board members, William Patton (a planning guru in his own right, with a Ph.D. in systems planning), then combines the answers, eliminating repetitive responses. Then the six get together and talk about the substance of the comments, hashing out a common list of mission aims and ranking them in order of importance. This "mission statement" becomes the backbone of the strategic plan, and the most widely disseminated piece of the plan: All employees have a copy in their handbooks, and it is given to all job applicants as an introduction to the company.

II. Future Direction

The second most important question to answer before beginning the planning process is "What is our future direction? Where do we want to be five or ten years from now?" The longer-term vision for the company feeds into shorter-term operational plans for day-to-day business. In order to develop an effective plan for the next 12 months, your company must have a very clear idea of where you want to be in the long term, say, five years in the future.

The following questions will help you create a collaborative definition of your company's future direction, which will serve as the framework for defining the 12-month strategic plan.

As you answer the following questions, imagine that you are describing your company five years in the future. The more detailed and specific you can get, the better you will be able to transfer those goals to the strategic plan. In turn, this will help you to clearly articulate the long-term goals and direction of the company.

- What is your market position and market share?
- What is your product/service mix?
- Who are your customers?
- What is your financial situation?
- What geographic areas is the company operating in?
- What is it like to work for the company at this time?
- What kind of reputation do we have, both in the marketplace and with the public?

On the basis of the answers to these questions, write down a description of the company in the future that combines the most important aspects from each. Try to keep the description concise: a paragraph or so.

III. Strategic Analysis

Third, review the marketplace and the specific strengths and weaknesses of the company as it stands today. This will lead to an assessment of the critical issues that the company must face and overcome in order to grow effectively. The standard format for analyzing your strategic business situation is called a SWOT analysis, standing for *strengths, weaknesses, opportunities,* and *threats.* Discussion of the following questions can provide the fundamental assumptions that undergird the planning process.

Strengths

- What are our greatest strengths?
- What has made our company successful?
- Why are customers using our services/products?

Weaknesses

- What is our company doing that is exceptionally *unsuccessful?*
- What are the characteristics of that lack of success?
- Why is it happening?

Opportunities

- What are the three greatest opportunities for the company over the next two years that will lead to our continued success?

Threats

- Who are our competitors? (Rank them.)
- What are the reasons customers would choose a competitor instead of us?
- What are the three greatest challenges facing the company over the next two years that we must overcome to ensure our continued success?

The SWOT analysis should lead to a discussion of the business's focus.

Focus

- What are the three most important areas of the business that will require excellence in order for the business to maintain its strength and to grow?

- What are the *most important* changes we must make this year in order to be successful?

Answering these questions will provide the platform from which you can begin writing the planning document itself. At any company, some of these issues will be more important than others. If, for example, you realize that sales are topping out in existing markets, diversification may be a valid strategy. If changes in existing markets will broaden sales possibilities, it may not be immediately essential to look for new products and markets.

EXAMPLE OF SWOT ANALYSIS BY A $2 MILLION PUBLIC RELATIONS FIRM IN THE MIDWEST

Strengths

- Strong sense of mission and vision; serious about success
- Excellent core staff
- Strong leadership at the top
- Excellent communication systems in place
- Morale is excellent
- Commitment to communicating with clients and responding to needs
- The firm is financially sound
- Demonstrated commitment and interest in the community

Weaknesses

- Making promises to prospective clients that we can't deliver
- Duplication of efforts
- Lack of ongoing training and budget to implement
- Lack of company manuals on operations procedures
- Need for administrative assistant
- Lack of state-of-the-art file-tracking system

- Lack of retirement program to help with retention of key personnel
- Need more effective criteria for hiring
- Not enough space to accommodate the number of people needed
- Need for more delegation
- Lack of timely follow-through on commitments made to the staff

Opportunities

- Increase cash flow by more efficiently moving cases from start to finish
- Strength of current marketplace—expand locations
- Fine-tune systems to increase efficiency, which would lead to greater morale, better client satisfaction, and better cash flow
- Facilitate growth in new markets through acquisition
- Advertising is in place to create market share in a short period of time
- Growth of personnel through training
- Taking seminars to schools
- Start advertising agency
- Add partners with expertise and a client base

Threats

- No heir apparent to replace CEO
- Lack of operations director to facilitate growth
- Lack of human resources department to effectively recruit, orient, and train staff
- Lack of uniformity of policies between offices
- Inability to find qualified personnel to expand growth
- Unwillingness of partners to reduce their shares in order to bring in additional partners
- Prospect of burnout for staff as work load increases
- Growing too fast

- Possible over-extension of the firm financially
- Inability to maintain company culture while continuing to expand

IV. Writing the Plan

Now you are ready to commit to writing specific strategies and activities that will be most important for your company to achieve in the next 12 months. The planning itself starts with a focus on broad strategic goals, and then funnels down to specific operational tactics to ensure the execution of the strategies. It basically involves the following format:

1. Develop core objectives.

Based on the previous discussions, information gathered, and the identification of the most critical issues for the company, develop the core objectives for the strategic plan. Core objectives should be broad, general targets or goals that the business will achieve in the next 12 months, consistent with the purpose and long-term vision for the company. These should not be too detailed; instead, only major issues that will impact the company's progress should be identified.

What key goals or targets do you want to achieve in the next 12 months?

Examples:

- Increase revenues by 25 percent
- Become market leaders in certain niche
- Improve profitability to 10 percent
- Streamline operations
- Get a marketing department in place

2. Develop strategies for each objective.

Strategy is the overall game plan for achieving objectives. Strategies provide the direction for everyone in setting department and individual goals for the coming year. Brainstorm 5 to 15 strategies for each core objective. Then prioritize and identify the top 2 to 4 strategies for each objective.

Examples:

- Expand internationally (to increase revenue by 25 percent)
- Increase utilization of existing customer base (to increase revenue)

- Focus on the most profitable products/services (to improve profitability)
- Establish inventory management system (to streamline operations)

3. Develop tactics and action plans.

The strategy must be translated into specific, measurable, and dated tactics. Tactics are step-by-step action plans for achieving the strategies, with names and dates attached to each action item. Without this follow-through, the strategy will be nothing more than a mental exercise that will have very little likelihood of ever being achieved. Each department should set up straightforward and clear operational plans to implement the strategies. Make specific, dated, measurable statements of who does what for each strategy, and when each will be accomplished. For each department, the five key components of tactics are the following:

- Meeting the objective
- The measurable outcomes (what exactly will be done)
- The time frame
- The cost
- Who will be held responsible

4. Monitor and follow through.

It is the responsibility of the CEO to monitor progress on the plan, to make sure that the activities and priorities are carried out in a timely manner by the accountable parties. The tactical action plans will provide a benchmark for performance. The CEO should meet with the management team on a monthly basis to track execution. Having a written document helps with accountability, since each person knows what is expected of him or her, and the key indicators for performance have been agreed upon by everyone.

For example, Harlan Accola, former CEO of Skypix, in Marshfield, Wisconsin, used a three-page report each Thursday to monitor progress on his company's plan. The report listed weekly sales, accounts payable and receivable, cash balances, inventory levels, and leads generated. "It was a pulse point" said Accola. And it was the vehicle by which the company compared performance against the plan.

At Dura-Line Corp., a manufacturer of extruded plastic pipes based in Middleboro, Kentucky, the planning process revealed that two of its newest geographic markets, the United Kingdom and the West Coast, were going to grow dramatically. The then-owner, John Shoffner, recognized a need to broaden the company's product line and customer base beyond the already crowded and competitive business of portable water piping. That led to some pretty specific operational questions: Would it be best for the company to buy or build production facilities in the United Kingdom and California? What kind of staffing increases would be necessary and cost-justified? Was the company's sales team adequate to meet its growth goals? Was tax planning adequate? Was cash flow at its maximum? If so, could it finance growth activities?

New planners must also be prepared for those agonizing moments when operational answers reveal that certain strategic goals are impractical, at least over a middle term. More frequently, planning forces companies to rank their growth goals and strategies.

Consider Dura-Line's experience: Shoffner knew that he needed to acquire or build two new facilities in order to reach his new target markets. But given the limits on his own time and management support, he realized that he would have to tackle one expansion at a time. After a few conversations with Tom Quinn, president of Dura-Line's parent company, Jordan Industries, in Chicago, he decided it made sense to go after the United Kingdom first, where demand for his product was already so strong that it was distracting Dura-Line from other clients.

"Reality" is the key word to remember when talking about business planning. All the theory and questions and answers in the world mean nothing if the planning process doesn't produce real-life results: faster growth, higher profit margins, better customer service.

SUMMARY: 10 REASONS WHY PLANNING WORKS

Strategic planning increases the effectiveness of an organization's growth in at least ten ways.

1. Planning forces you to define the future direction for the company in terms of *measurable results.*

It's one thing to set a vision for a glorious future for your company, and quite another to actually pull it off. Planning forces you to take that ideal destination and break it down to a quantifiable set of activities that, taken step by step, will move the company progressively toward the goal.

2. Planning ensures that the company maintains a strategic *focus*.

Entrepreneurial companies are known for their tendency to take on whatever the market hands to them—as long as there's money to be made. This is not always in the best long-term interest of the business; many companies have woken up to find themselves in so many different businesses that they no longer do any one thing very well. Strategic planning forces you to evaluate each business decision to ensure that it is aligned with your predetermined purpose and direction for the company.

3. Planning allows time for *contemplation and reflection*.

Most entrepreneurs are so busy running the business that they barely have time for lunch, much less strategic-level thinking. But thinking is important, and at times more important than the daily activities that are driving the business. Planning forces the leadership team to take time out, away from the rigors and demands of everyday work, to think about the business from a different point of view, to make decisions that will have a lasting impact.

4. Planning prioritizes the issues that must be addressed to achieve corporate goals.

Running a business by the seat of the pants is not the most likely path to growth. The stark reality of most growth companies is that priorities are driven by crisis—the squeaky wheel gets the oil. Without any real priorities set down by the management team, the business will meander from fire to fire and never get momentum going in any particular direction. The planning process allows you to assess the realities of the current situation and draw consensus on what the priorities are for long-term growth and success. Having clear priorities keeps everyone on track with decisions about what's really important.

5. Planning guides effective decision-making and validates *allocation of time* for each manager and employee.

Once priorities are in place via the planning process, corporate objectives trickle down into clearly defined actions for each department, manager, and employee. As a result, each person in the organization knows how his or her work contributes to achieving the overall corporate goals.

6. Planning allows you to be proactive rather than reactive and *anticipate the right opportunities.*

With a strategic focus and clear priorities in place, the company is in a position to keep a sharp lookout for new opportunities that fit. Planning, therefore, is a tool that can make a company more flexible because it provides the structure and framework for assessing new decisions and incorporating them into the overall strategy.

7. Planning provides a tool for *monitoring progress.*

Planning produces a quantifiable set of actions and measurable outcomes, which can be used as a benchmark for achieving your goals. This provides a clear-cut approach for managing a company's growth, with clearly defined activities and results to measure performance by.

8. Planning is a *means of communication* for the entire company.

Many CEOs think that ad hoc conversations with different managers as they pass in the hallway will keep them informed and keyed into the corporate goals, strategies, and overall direction. Not true. Especially as a company grows, it becomes increasingly important to communicate clearly to all employees the overall strategy and direction of the company, and how each person's activities are contributing to that future direction. Strategic planning provides a vehicle for communicating this information in a concrete manner to avoid miscommunication and uncertainties regarding performance expectations.

9. Planning gets everyone moving in the same direction.

Strategic planning allows for a coordinated process to streamline activities and decisions toward the same end result. With a clearly communicated plan, people at all levels in the organization understand the company's goals and direction and will stay in step.

10. Planning facilitates *cross-functional connections* between departments.

As a business grows and distinct departments and divisions emerge, the tendency is for each to begin operating independently with its own agenda and priorities. This is almost a natural result of organizational development and the resulting delegation of roles, responsibilities, tasks, and lines of authority. Strategic planning prevents the potential fragmentation of different departments by bringing together department managers and staff to work together to develop a common view of corporate goals and strategies. Once they understand the full picture, department leaders will have a better understanding of how all areas function together to achieve corporate goals.

CHAPTER 7

Internal Infrastructure

IN THE PHYSICAL ENVIRONMENT, A GOOD INFRASTRUCTURE —roads, bridges, traffic lights—ensures that people can travel smoothly to their destination. Without these structures, it would be much more difficult to get from one place to another: There would be more accidents, people would get stuck, breakdowns would frequently occur. In business, the Internal Infrastructure represents the systems and procedures that allow information and communication to flow smoothly throughout the organization. It also supports the company's strategy and allows people to perform their jobs effectively.

Internal Infrastructure can be an extremely open-ended subject, since so many different kinds of requirements for systems and procedures are found in each business. In every business, a myriad of nuances and unique situations impact the Internal Infrastructure needs, which include the stage of growth of the business, the level of professional staff, the number of employees, the technical proficiency, the type of industry, the geographical location, and the physical sites. All of these influence the kind of systems that may or may not be in place at any particular time. This chapter focuses on the fundamental areas that every business must deal with at the key points of transition as it grows.

In the previous chapters, the focus was not on daily business operations but on long-term and externally-oriented issues. Gathering Market Intelligence requires that you be externally focused instead of getting too bogged down in operations. One of the key points in Strategic Leadership is for the business owner to shift his or her focus from the daily details to long-range strategic thinking. Clarity of Purpose spotlights a company's sense of identity. And Strategic Planning is a process for translating your future goals for the business into specific action steps.

When we zero in on internal infrastructure, however, the daily reality of business becomes the focus. This is where the rubber meets the road, as they say.

There is a reason why Internal Infrastructure is the last of the five Growth Drivers to be discussed. Most businesses naturally focus their attention in this area, often at the expense of the "big picture." We've all heard managers say, "We can't see the forest for the trees"; day-to-day business operations become so urgent and consuming that managers' attention is diverted from the long-term strategic issues. Every day there are real issues to deal with as you manage your company—problems that must be solved and products or services that must get delivered to customers. Although these are obviously important, the longer-term issues have been addressed first in this book because they are often neglected, and are difficult to focus on while a company is growing. Consequently, there tends to be a natural imbalance in the amount of attention Infrastructure issues receive. That is why we send Internal Infrastructure to "the back of the line."

Often, however, infrastructure issues genuinely take priority over the longer-term issues, especially for businesses in Stage 2, "rapid growth." Many companies go through their initial stages of growth without paying much attention to systems, standards, or operating procedures. This is especially true when the entrepreneur insists on maintaining control over all the details of the business, makes all decisions, and resists delegation. In these situations, the neglected Infrastructure becomes a constraint on continued growth. If it is ignored or its importance underestimated, a company will grow as long as the infrastructure supports the business. Then it will implode. This is a common cause of death for many promising companies. In those cases, establishing a sound Internal Infrastructure is the most critical priority for growth and should take priority over long-term issues.

Norm Brodsky had a fast-growth company back in the 1980s that went from $0 to $120 million in seven years. Fourteen months later, the company wound up in Chapter 11. On hindsight, Brodsky sees where he went wrong. "The company needed management, stability, and structure, and I kept it from getting them. I was so desperate to sustain the head rush of start-up chaos that I made a hasty series of bad acquisitions. I made all the final decisions and didn't let the managers do their jobs. In the end, I paid a steep price."

The main problem with a company that has outgrown its Internal Infrastructure is a lack of clear policies and systems for making decisions and executing them. As a result, the company behaves in a more and more unpredictable manner. Every new business situation that arises is handled differently, by a different person. Or, the problem ends up going back to the CEO because no one knows how to make the right decision. This ad hoc operational style generally forces the CEO to become more and more controlling. He will feel the need to be involved in every decision, because no one else is capable of making the same quality of decisions he can. Of course, they can't because they have never been given the structure or policies to make those decisions.

As a company makes the transition from a start-up to an established organization, it requires management disciplines that were not necessary in the start-up stage: order, structure, and predictability. Employees experiencing the transition from start-up to rapid growth desperately want these structures and systems. They want to know what to expect every day when they walk into the office. They want predictability and order. People need to know what the rules are, instead of dealing with each situation on an ad hoc basis. The development of business disciplines and an administrative system is key to building Infrastructure and entering the next stage of development. A growing company needs to establish controls and decentralized decision-making at all levels in the business, in financial, operational, and organizational areas.

INTERNAL INFRASTRUCTURE LINKED TO PLANNING

The planning process is where tactical issues of Internal Infrastructure naturally emerge, as the management team takes broad objectives and breaks them down into specific action plans. The process itself generally brings to light gaps or weaknesses in the company's Internal Infrastructure, and spotlights the need to address them. For instance, it may become clear through the planning process that you need to hire new staff, invest in new technology, reorganize for growth, or clean up some of the business processes. When the planning process reveals that the systems and structures are not in place to support the strategy, those systems must be created; otherwise it will be extremely difficult for a company to achieve its growth goals.

There are three crucial indicators of a need to focus on short-term operational issues rather than long-term planning: (1) if a company's customer service is deteriorating; (2) if the quality of its products is declining; or (3) if there is a lack of accurate financial information. The first two areas are important because if a company cannot maintain a satisfactory level of customer service or quality, it simply cannot compete in today's marketplace. When quality and service are slipping, it is usually a sign of deeper infrastructure problems, such as technology that cannot handle current sales volume; staff that are not properly hired, trained, or managed; or recurring mistakes that are caused by a lack of appropriate business systems. The third critical area that supersedes long-term planning is a lack of financial information. A company that is operating without accurate financial data cannot make good strategic or operational decisions because it cannot determine the financial implications of those decisions. By the time the company realizes this, it may be too late.

COMPONENTS OF INFRASTRUCTURE

A company's Internal Infrastructure can generally be broken down into three components: organizational structure (who's doing what); business systems (how things get done); and financial controls (how the resources are managed). And overarching these three components are performance *metrics:* business performance indicators that allow management to measure and monitor corporate performance.

Organizational Structure

A company cannot achieve its growth potential if the roles and responsibilities for each employee are not clearly defined. Organizational structure answers the question "Who does what?" Specifically, it says who is responsible for each task and function within the organization, and how roles and responsibilities are defined. For many companies as they grow, the organizational structure evolves on its own rather than following a master design. It's easy to see how that happens, because the growth of a company causes gradual increases in complexity rather than clear-cut transitions. When the company is small, employees are hired as needed and generally are expected to wear a lot of different hats and pitch in whenever necessary. Lines of authority, communication, and delegation are not big issues, because everyone works in very close proximity with one another and can exchange information easily. It's like one big happy family.

But as the company grows, more employees are added, often without thought as to how they fit with other employees. As the physical space expands, people become spread out among different offices. They see each other less often and are not even sure what kind of work others are doing. Over time you end up with a company whose organizational structure either makes no sense or looks like a convoluted spider web. People may have been given a specific title, but they are still expected to chip in wherever there are gaps. Performance expectations are fuzzy. Employees are not sure exactly who their boss is. Every situation seems to require a different model for making decisions. "It depends . . ." is the answer to many operational and organizational questions. There is one "key person" who must be involved in every decision. If an outsider asks an employee, "So, what is your job and specific responsibility here?," the employee replies with a hesitation and a smirk—because there is no delineation of roles and responsibilities, causing a sense of ambiguity.

With a smaller number of employees, the ambiguity is necessary, and is possibly even a competitive weapon. The early-growth company is expected to be agile and flexible in order to cope, compete, and outmaneuver the big guys. Having a loosely structured organization reduces bureaucracy and increases flexibility and response time for making decisions. But when the business grows and the number of employees is counted in the dozens, it's time to get organized. For the business to run in an orderly fashion, people must clearly understand their specific roles.

EXERCISE: HOW ORGANIZED IS YOUR ORGANIZATION?

Decide whether the following statements are true or false. Then add up the total number of "true" and "false" answers.

1. We have an organizational chart on paper that we often refer to. True___ False___

2. We have written job descriptions for employees.
True___ False___

3. We have a company manual for policies and procedures.
   True___ False___

4. Performance evaluations are routine for every employee.
   True___ False___

5. The CEO is not generally involved in making operational
   decisions.   True___ False___

6. Lines of authority are clear—employees know exactly whom
   they report to, and they rarely circumvent their manager.
   True___ False___

7. People clearly understand their responsibilities and performance expectations.   True___ False___

8. Mediocrity, poor performance, and defiance are not tolerated.
   True___ False___

9. People generally know who is responsible for what throughout
   the organization.   True___ False___

10. New employees go through a routine orientation and training
    program.   True___ False___

TOTAL: TRUE___   FALSE___

SCORING

If you answered "True" to eight or more questions, your company
is well organized and has the structures in place to grow effectively.

If you answered "True" to four to seven questions, your company
has made some efforts in setting up an organizational structure,
but needs improvement.

If you answered "True" to less than four questions, your company
has very little organizational structure. This will hold back future
growth, particularly if you already have 20 or more employees.
The development of an organizational structure should be a priority for your business.

How to Approach Organizational Structure

When it's time to reorganize (or if you are developing your company's first *real* organizational structure), it is important to organize
around functions and tasks rather than people. In other words, people

must be assigned to tasks and functions on the basis of their competence rather than of their availability. If your company is serious about growth, you must work hard to make sure you have the right people in the right place doing the right job.

For example, the owners of a Los Angeles clothing distributor decided it was time to develop specific job descriptions and titles for each employee, after they had grown to 50 employees. Employees were complaining that work was becoming too confusing, because it was unclear who was responsible for what. To address this problem, the owners spent hours interviewing employees, then asked them to write down what they thought their jobs were. But when they compiled the information and tried to build an organizational chart based on the data, it made no sense. There were no connections—they had a group of individuals, all doing their own work in their own way. Roles and responsibilities were based on employees' perception of their jobs, rather than on the jobs that needed to be done.

It would have made more sense for this company to approach the organizational structure by first observing essential work flow, functions, and tasks, and then defining the most sensible organization to accomplish those. Then they should clarify the specific functions necessary for the business to operate effectively. Instead, they were asking employees what *they* thought they would like to do in their jobs.

An organizational chart should organize business functions in a way that facilitates the company's effective operation. Once constructed, the structure provides a working model for staffing the company (either adding to or removing current staff), because it forces the company to look at the important jobs that need to be filled, rather than on the people that are available.

Once job descriptions for each manager and employee are clear, the next step is to set up formal evaluation procedures to assess performance on a regular basis.

Management Talent

If a company wants to grow, it must invest in the appropriate management talent and depth to support its growth goals. Sometimes that talent exists within the company, other times it must come from outside. In most cases, CEOs find that their companies eventually outgrow the home-grown managers. What to do with a manager who has been with the company since the beginning but doesn't have the skills to operate on the next level becomes a difficult decision. The owner may think of these managers as part of their family and feel obligated to keep them on the payroll. This gets further complicated when managers have been given promotions or higher-level titles, but the CEO continues to step in and make decisions for them. That problem is often due to a lack of trust in the manager by the CEO. The antidote is to hire trustworthy leaders and managers whom the CEO respects enough to give them the power and authority to do their job.

This dilemma is a common issue for many companies on the growth curve. When is it appropriate to hire professional managers instead of promoting "home-grown" managers? It's not an easy question to answer. There are some general rules of thumb for grappling with these decisions. If a company has a strong philosophy regarding internal promotion, and has an effective and extensive management training program in place, then promoting from within can work well.

ABC Supply Co. is a good example of this philosophy's success. ABC, based in Beloit, Wisconsin, boasts $950 million in sales and 2,300 employees. It is a national chain of wholesale construction-supply out-lets that earned the number one spot on the 1986 *Inc.* 500 list, when it had 600 employees and $183 million in revenues.

CEO Ken Hendricks doesn't want to spend too much of his time in the stores managing customers—he wants to hire others to do it, peo-ple who would think and act like him. "I never did spend a lot of time in the stores," he says. Knowing that store floors weren't where he want-ed to plant his feet gave him an incentive to think hard about training. "You hire people and train them to care about customers," he says. He spends his time talking to his managers, training them to think like owners, and giving them the psychic and financial rewards they need to run their individual businesses. He has hired trainers from Domino's Pizza and Marriott International, hosts an annual five-day training ses-sion and awards banquet to honor top performers, provides managers with monthly financial statements for their stores, and teaches them how to read and interpret the numbers. And at year's end, Hendricks distributes 25 percent of the company's pretax profits to employees according to the profitability of individual stores—an incentive system that has rewarded some truckdrivers and warehouse staff with bonuses in the $3,000 to $8,000 range. This structure has rewarded Hendricks handsomely over the years; his company has hit the *Inc.* 500 list three times so far.

Unlike ABC, many growth companies tend to take the path of least resistance (and least investment) when it comes to management development. They don't have a management training program, and think that it's cheaper and easier to promote that smart young front-line person to supervisor status, rather than spend the big bucks on a seasoned professional. Then that bright but inexperienced person is expected to grow and develop spontaneously in tandem with the company. Sometimes it works out, particularly if a company is not growing very quickly and the environment doesn't change much over time. But when a company is growing at a rapid pace, chances are that putting an inexperienced, untrained individual in a management position will fail. The home-grown manager will face new and complex challenges without appropriate skills and experience to draw from.

If you intend to groom existing employees to fill management positions as the company grows, make sure that you invest in their professional development and personal growth. Send them to professional trade groups, seminars, meetings, and local business schools. If you truly expect your people to grow and perform in step with the company's growth, do what it takes to support and develop them.

For those companies on a more aggressive growth track, it is best to bring on professional managers who have the experience, qualifications, and skills to grow the company. This is usually a wise investment in the future of the business. Ideally, hire managers who are smarter than you in their respective disciplines. Also make sure that you are considering candidates who have been involved in entrepreneurial growth companies. Whether it was a success or a failure is less important—a good manager will bring valuable experiences from both. In some cases, problem situations have arisen when entrepreneurs of small growth companies have hired executives from *Fortune* 500 companies, only to end up with a culture clash. These executives expected certain perks and cushy management benefits that came with the territory in a big company. But it doesn't work that way in an *Inc.* 500 company, does it? A company car? Forget it. Golf outings on Friday afternoons? Sorry, there's work to be done. How about having that annual meeting in St. Croix? Unlikely. Instead, hire managers with an entrepreneurial ethic—they understand growth, they can make things happen, they want compensation tied to results, and they know how to work with and get alliance from the other managers as well as the front line staff.

Harlan Accola, for example, wanted to grow his Wisconsin aerial photography business from its sales of roughly $2 million, but he knew that the business still had a ragged feel to it. It had a computer system with powerful software and nobody who knew how to run it. The lead-generation and telemarketing area, a core of the business, was weak. Accola wasn't well versed in interpreting financial information and the business wasn't making much money.

Accola took the critical step of bringing in an accountant who had been controller of a company that, in 12 years, had grown from $3 million to $50 million and was sold to Kraft General Foods. The accountant was looking for a small company at which he could make a difference. His experience matched Accola's needs, so Accola brought him in as an equity partner with a one-third share. "We wanted to keep him around for the long term," Accola says. He rounded out the team by hiring a data-processing expert and a telemarketing specialist. Within two years, the company's revenues reached $4.7 million and after-tax profits rose to about 7 percent (up from 4.9 percent).

Unite Department Managers on Corporate Goals and Strategy

Once the right management team is on board, it is important for the managers to be clear on corporate goals, strategy, and direction. If the CEO does not communicate the overall direction and strategy for the company, department managers will end up evolving toward independence with their own agendas. This issue of "management disintegration" occurs frequently in many companies followed by *Inc.* Without a clearly communicated plan, turf wars will begin to erupt because departments are unclear about distribution of resources and priorities. Individual agendas are given a higher priority than corporate goals because corporate goals are unclear.

Compensation and Incentive Programs

Does your receptionist have a production quota? There is an old saying, "You get what you measure." At successful growth companies, every employee has a quantifiable goal to meet. It is essential that growth companies establish the connection between employee or department performance and compensation. Compensation is a fundamental business tool that allows managers to perform in a manner consistent with corporate goals. It is an effective method for ensuring a focus on goals throughout the organization, and should be seriously considered once the company has determined its corporate objectives and specific strategies. (There are many books on this topic, some of which are suggested in the Resources section in Chapter 8.)

Perry Klebahn, CEO of $4.8 million Atlas Snow-Shoe Co., in San Francisco, has set up his company so that all employees have some of their compensation tied to a quantitative goal specific to his or her job. The sales staff have order quotas. The line workers in manufacturing strive to minimize "hours per person per pair" of snowshoes. Even the receptionist has a goal: to send out 50 of the company's catalogs each day. "I want to be able to measure everything," says Klebahn. "It drives people nuts, but if we can't measure it, we can't improve it."

Employee Handbook

There comes a time in every company's growth when an employee manual is essential. For Bulbtronics, in Farmingdale, New York, according to Executive Vice-President Susan Winters, that time came about five years ago, when the bulb distributor—now at more than 80 employees—got to the 25- to 30-person mark and policies had to be standardized. Until then, personnel policies were decided on an ad hoc basis. "But at sixty, fifty, even forty employees, you are better off with something that has no ambiguities," Winters says.

Winters, who runs Bulbtronics's operations, says people always had the same questions: What were the hours of operation? What was the vacation policy? When were they entitled to benefits? Finally, she realized there were too many "little things that may not have been communicated—but I didn't want people to know after the fact."

It is generally good advice to create an employee handbook once the number of employees exceeds 25 or so. Other than maybe your tax returns, you can't prepare a more important document. An employee handbook is a place where you can say exactly who you are and what you do. (One handbook refers to itself as a "sort of a yearly corporate manifesto.") Most important, your handbook tells employees why they should work for your company; it should detail your expectations of them and answer their expectations of you. In other words, it will provide clearly documented policies for personnel to follow. Like it or not, as the company grows the likelihood of unfair, illegal, miscommunicated, or uncontrolled personnel issues will increase and become more and more of a potential liability. An employee handbook is necessary to cover legal requirements and avoid lawsuits. It is simply prudent risk management.

An employee handbook should achieve the following for your company:

1. Communicate indispensable company policies and practices.

2. Make explicit the mutual agreements between employee and employer without being an actual contract.

3. State a company's philosophy.

4. Excite and motivate the employee about his or her job.

5. Convey a broader sense of the company mission.

Many handbooks start by stating the company's core purpose, followed with a brief history of the company. Your handbook is the place to walk the talk. The Wild Oats Company's *Staff Handbook*, a 48-page guide, contains such chapters as "Responsibility to Our Customers," "Responsibility to Our Staff," as well as "Nuts and Bolts." All the philosophy in the world doesn't mean a thing unless the employee manual's tenets are firmly embedded in the company's human-resources policy and evidenced by its practices.

Good handbooks strike a tone that is welcoming and authoritative yet use language that's crystal clear. Bad ones are filled with intimidating discourses on policy and lists of thou-shalt-nots, in unintelligible and uninviting legalese. "I want the handbook to feel like the advice of somebody who has worked here for ten years telling me what it's like to work here," says Joe Mansueto, CEO of the 200-employee Chicago-based financial publisher Morningstar Mutual Funds. Like Wild Oats' handbook, the company's guide has a collegial, informal tone consistent with the company culture. This section, for instance, sports a breezy, direct tone that speaks volumes:

> Chill out! It's very hard, if not impossible, to provide great service
> if you are stressed out, so be good to yourself. Find ways to ease
> the tension and stress of daily work. Bring some toys to the office,
> get out for a short walk, listen to some favorite music, take the

time to eat a good meal or even just spend a few minutes breathing deeply.

From reading the handbook employees should know what kind of company they are working for. Following purpose and history, the essential sections are:

Employment policies. Basic information on issues such as equal employment opportunity, job postings, work hours, regular and overtime pay, performance reviews, vacations and holidays, personal and sick days, leaves of absence, and jury duty.

Benefits. The fundamental provisions on issues such as health, dental, and life insurance, short-term and long-term disability, workers' compensation, retirement programs, tuition reimbursement, and employee-assistance programs.

Employee conduct. Information on themes as specific as employee hygiene or the company's dress code and as broad as individual development.

Organization chart. The company's handbook should give people a sense of where they fit in to the organization. Some handbooks give the names of company officers and departments and the chain of command; others may provide a map of the premises. Others list the phone numbers (sometimes home numbers as well) of every employee.

Legal stuff. This is where the handbook gets serious. First of all, companies must include several statements on specific laws. The Family and Medical Leave Act policy must be in a company handbook, which must also contain a written sexual-harassment policy, and, in some cases, a smoking or nonsmoking policy. There is also a section on dispute resolution. The list varies from state to state.

Avoid lawsuits by avoiding the most common mistake: policies that are not drafted clearly. For example, a handbook may refer to a policy for "all employees," when such benefits may be only for full-timers.

One final note: When establishing company systems for the first time, an important element of success will be the owners' setting a good example. In short, your own behavior must reflect the administrative and operational decisions and policies that are established. It won't work if the owners fail to follow the policies that they set.

Business Systems

The development of business disciplines and an administrative system is key to making the transition from one level of growth to the next. Business systems are found in every area of the business—in each function, behind every decision and each transaction. The systems are the answer to the question "How do things get done?" What is the procedure for setting up a new account? What process takes place from the time an order is received to the point where it is shipped out to the customer? How are customer complaints resolved? How is the telephone answered? Business systems provide consistent standards and structures for the organization's performance. They also eliminate the danger of relying on any one person's knowledge for making decisions, and allow business functions to be replicated and followed by anyone.

Business systems can be applied to something as simple as how one answers the phone. In a customer service department, for example, there may be a systematic method for answering the phone before the third ring. The phone is answered in the same manner regardless of who picks up ("Thank you for calling XYZ company! This is Janice. How may I help you?"). Customers perceive a consistently positive and friendly tone from the company, and employees have specific standards for doing their job.

At the other extreme, business systems can also be applied to the organization as a whole, with the application of enterprise resource planning (ERP) systems. These enormously complex software systems generally provide a business with seamless integration of virtually all information that flows through a company—financial, accounting, sales and marketing, operations, logistics, and human resources. Implementation of these software systems requires a great deal of money, time, and expertise, but the upside is the efficiencies and improved quality achieved through company-wide compatibility. In other words, each person in each department—sales and ordering, production and scheduling, financial reporting, and customer service—is talking the same language and using the same system.

Lane Nemeth, the founder of Discovery Toys, now in Livermore, California, confronted the issue of growing a company without company-wide operational standards when her chief operations officer died after ten years of employment. The COO had complete control of the operational side of the business, an area Lane simply didn't care for. Not long after his death, Nemeth decided that Discovery Toys should branch out into children's clothing, and she launched into the project with her usual focus on design and market research. Although the clothing line was successful in terms of quality and customer satisfaction, it created many new problems in the warehousing and inventory arenas which caused frustration and concern among the company's sales reps. Lane had never analyzed the project implications from an operations perspective. As a result, she pulled the plug on the clothing line after a year, taking significant losses.

It was clear to Lane that relying on just one person for all the corporate knowledge of operations was not appropriate as the company was growing from $37.9 million in 1986 to current sales of more than $100 million. She had hoped there were systems in place to provide some kind of framework for analyzing and monitoring operational activities, but there wasn't—it was all in the COO's head. "If your organization is dependent on one person, you're in trouble," she says. Nemeth is now intent on making sure that her top managers understand the entire business and are putting the systems in place to manage it more effectively.

A lack of business systems will stifle growth.

Weak systems can become a stumbling block to many entrepreneurs as they move through the early stages of growth. Often the business owner is a technical genius or a sales champion rather than an administrator. Many entrepreneurs lack the interest or aptitude to spend much time on the boring details of operations. As a result, no one in the company is really responsible for paying attention to the operations of the business. The company continues to grow, but the systems do not keep pace with the growth, and the business becomes increasingly vulnerable to breakdowns and operational crises. If not addressed, inadequate business systems will hold back the company's growth because the Infrastructure simply cannot handle any more volume. One crisis could wipe out the entire business. The ability of a company to operate a finely tuned, well-managed business with excellence will have a crucial impact on its ability to compete in the marketplace and succeed in achieving its growth goals.

Many companies reach a key juncture where the business systems are one of the most critical factors for the company's long-term success. If they lack formal systems, standards, and operating procedures for various functions of the business, they will encounter more and more problems. If Internal Infrastructure is the weakest area for your company (as shown by the Growth Strategy Analysis), it will become extremely important to have an executive in place to establish the appropriate administrative systems and controls. A pro-active, accountable leader must do the job of instituting and managing a company's operational systems. The business founder-entrepreneur, who is generally not interested in the administrative details of the business, is usually not appropriate for the job. But a good chief operating officer, general manager, or controller–chief financial officer may be the right person to initiate the necessary changes and standards throughout the organization. Each business must determine the best time to bring on an executive-level second-in-command, but it would be especially important if a company is experiencing rapid growth, business systems are weak, and the business founder has no interest in administration.

Norm Brodsky knew he was not the ideal candidate for building the administrative structure needed to take his document-management company called CitiStorage in Brooklyn, New York, to the next level of growth. He had learned this lesson from the failure of his previous company which went bankrupt owing to lack of Infrastructure. He admittedly prefers chaos: the thrill of crisis management—always on the firing line—juggling a dozen balls without letting any of them drop. Everyone depends on you. "No one questions your decision-making process," Brodsky says. "You're almost like a god in that situation and you run on pure adrenaline. I love every minute of it." To Brodsky, professional management was a bore. He didn't have the patience for it, nor the interest in discussing how things ought to be done. But that's exactly what the business needed.

So Brodsky looked for someone else to manage the transition from chaos to an orderly management system—a professional manager who could create stability through planning, organization, and commitment. One who found building companies as exciting as he found starting them. He ended up hiring a friend who was perfectly qualified, whom he trusted, and who had previously built and sold seven companies. The results? Employee turnover is way down. The accounting department has done a complete turnaround. Most of the employees are thriving under the new regime.

Ximena Florez, president of MicroEdge in New York City, knew that her software development firm, which provides financial management software to nonprofit charitable trusts and foundations to help track donations, was growing beyond the scope of her management capacity. While her husband Dov headed up the technical aspects of the business, Florez ran sales, marketing, and operations. Sales growth was strong, about 30 percent a year for three years running, but it posed new problems.

"I knew that I was getting spread too thin," Florez says. "I needed to have someone else focus on the day-to-day operation so that I could continue concentrating on the strategic side." She became especially concerned that quality and customer support keep up with the growth of the customer base. "It's great to have our product in such demand in the market," says Ximena, "but our clients expect a high level of quality and support. If our service declines, word gets around pretty fast."

Florez spent an entire year searching before she found the right candidate to hire as chief operating officer. "He's been absolutely terrific," Florez says, with a mix of relief and excitement. "He started with customer support, and put in systems, goals and measurements so that we can constantly monitor our performance." Next he's turning to their information systems. Florez feels confident in the company's ability to manage the next level of growth.

Business systems and management: Let your managers manage.

As the company grows, business systems allow the CEO to strike a balance between freedom and control in overseeing the management team. Freedom cannot be given without responsibility, which is primarily a product of clearly defined roles and expectations for performance, and disciplined execution. If clear business controls are in place, they can be monitored on an ongoing basis. When there are no systems or controls, the tendency for many business owners is to control or get involved in decision-making at every level. Systems help to ensure that each business area is operating within a specific set of operational parameters. In order for the business to grow, it is imperative that managers have a clear understanding of controls so they can take responsibility for their actions.

Invest in technology.

As the company grows, information systems should not be ignored or underestimated as a strategic tool. Technology, a key leverage point for exploiting growth opportunities and maintaining competitive advantage, can play a significant role in a company's operations. It should be given a high profile and priority, because it will play a substantial role in the company's growth, competitiveness and profitability, and should be recognized as such.

The *Wall Street Journal* recently described the tale of an HMO that faced a financial crisis in large part due to growth that outpaced the organization's technology. Oxford Health Plans, Inc. was founded in the mid-1980s by entrepreneur Stephen Wiggins, with the intention of bringing managed care to the most difficult market in America— upscale doctors and consumers in metropolitan New York. He succeeded by bending all the rules in the HMO industry: offering a wide choice of physicians rather than limited access; paying medical providers generously rather than hounding them for discounts and cutbacks; offering the company's own network of alternative providers, such as massage therapists, chiropractors and the like; and offering members the opportunity to use out-of-network providers.

Wiggins used these innovative offerings to fuel growth. His maverick style and entrepreneurial drive built Oxford into a flourishing HMO that grew from 217,000 members in 1993 to nearly 2 million in 1997. But the same approach that was used to win these customers—offering them a wide variety of providers both inside and outside the HMO's network—was the very thing that caused the financial problems later on.

Maintaining control of the "out-of-network" care is difficult. Oxford found it to be increasingly challenging as the numbers of members grew beyond its in-house computer system's ability to handle them. But in spite of the clear signals that the data infrastructure was weak, Wiggins publicly insisted that there were no problems, and continued to focus on growth. "Ultimately Oxford lost control of its most basic billing and payment operations," reported the *Wall Street Journal*, "unaware that its Medicare costs were rising far higher than anticipated and unable to pay doctors and hospitals for up to a year or more in many cases." In October 1997 the company finally crashed, taking a 60 percent dive in its stock.

The management team at Oxford was so out of touch with the computer system's problems that a first draft of third-quarter results showed a healthy increase in profits of more than 45 percent. But upon closer examination, the numbers revealed a dramatic loss of $78.2 million for the quarter. As the news got out to Wall Street, the market value dropped more than $3.3 million overnight. Wiggins himself, the biggest investor, lost more than $115 million that day. He has since stepped down from his role as chairman, and a new CEO has been named to take the helm in an attempt to turn things around.

Contrast Oxford with Fisher SpacePen, a company that illustrates the powerful results that can be reaped from investing in technology and systems. Paul Fisher, now 85, the company's founder and CEO, found sales and profits languishing in the 1980s—a result of his resistance to getting involved with the information technology that was becoming the norm at other, faster-moving companies. It was as if Fisher SpacePen were in a time warp. But thanks to two persistent children and a fast-talking consultant, Fisher finally, if reluctantly, agreed to a high-tech makeover. The result is a stunning turnaround—in 1995 and 1996, sales increased by more than $2 million and in 1997, they hit $7.5 million.

Paul Fisher was an economist and an inveterate tinkerer when, in 1948, he decided to make a business of his obsession with designing a better ballpoint pen. Fisher Pen Co. thrived when it made smooth-writing ink cartridges, but it was the 1960s space race that inspired Fisher's crowning achievement: a pressurized pen that could write under almost any conditions, including zero gravity and vacuum. The pen became standard issue for astronauts, and thanks to the national space craze, Fisher was able to parlay NASA's seal of approval into a bonanza for mass-market versions of the SpacePen. Annual sales were around $6 million by the early 1970s, when Fisher renamed the business Fisher SpacePen Co.

But the magic of a NASA endorsement had worn off in the late 1970s, and there were no meteoric product innovations or down-to-earth marketing strategies waiting to replace it. As Fisher tried to fuel his company on the fizzling hype from the space craze, sales stayed flat, at around $7 million, through the early 1980s. Fisher's sons, Cary and Morgan, had entered the business by that time and had quickly recognized that the company's approach to marketing and finance was strictly from the *Sputnik* era. But their father refused to hear talk about new-fangled management tools. "He's a scientist, but he didn't trust computers," says Cary, who noted that his father's obsession with perfecting his ink formulas—to the senior Fisher, that was the only way to grow a successful pen company—got in the way of his making simple management decisions. "In one six-year period," Cary recalls, "my father didn't even raise prices."

And that's where things stood in 1994, when Jim Jobin stumbled across the Fisher SpacePen booth at an industry trade show. Jobin, 37, then director of marketing and national accounts for Perma Products, in Duncanville, Texas, had long been a fan of the SpacePen's never-fail functionality and offbeat elegance. (The most popular model resembles a rounded, large-caliber bullet; it snuggles comfortably in a pocket and uncaps to form a full-size pen.) Jobin started chatting with Morgan, who was running the booth. Soon Morgan, who had had hopes of growing the company quickly, was spilling his pent-up frustration at his father's slow-moving management style. Jobin and Morgan ended up talking for hours. Before long, Morgan offered him a job as a marketing consultant. Jobin couldn't resist. "I always carried a SpacePen in my shirt pocket," he laughs, "but I'd lost it." When Jobin stopped at the Fisher SpacePen booth, he had only been hoping to pick up a replacement.

After Jobin finally got a close look at the company's operations, he almost regretted his decision to join the team. Signs of old man Fisher's eccentricity were everywhere. For starters, the company location was Boulder City, Nevada—the only place in the state where gambling is illegal, and consequently a magnet for conservatives. And Fisher lives above the company's offices, erasing even that tiny gap that even the most ardent entrepreneurs usually maintain between their business and their personal life. But what really knocked Jobin for a loop was that nothing was automated. Other than a couple of stand-alone PCs and a primitive accounting program, there were few signs that the world had changed in the past quarter century. Jobin was so relieved to see a fax machine that he shuddered.

Lacking information technology, the sales operation was a mess. Leads were constantly falling through the cracks because the system for tracking them consisted of a notebook and some scraps of paper. With no way to organize leads by region, it wasn't unusual for a salesperson to travel to a state for just one sales call. Historical information was nil, making forecasting impossible. "The first year I was here, we lost four hundred thousand dollars because we miscalculated demand on certain products," says Jobin. The situation was so grim, Jobin realized, that he would have to put off his marketing mission. What this company needed first was a technical manager. Jobin was no techie, but he'd do what it took. "I had to," he says. "There was no Infrastructure."

The first challenge was bringing the senior Fisher into step. Fisher didn't seem to mind that the company had long since stopped growing; he liked running a small company. Clearly, Jobin wasn't going to win him over with talk of big plans. Instead, he wooed Fisher on the tennis courts (though Fisher often complained that Jobin let him win). Once he'd established trust on the clay, Jobin played to the older man's love of gadgetry, singing not the business but the technological praises of some of the newer computer products. Fisher eventually came through with a $35,000 computer budget—along with an offer of a full-time job as marketing director. (Jobin is now the owner of a three-store retail operation specializing in fine writing instruments, including Fisher's.)

Jobin went to work buying PCs and linking them via a Novell network. Unwilling to blow Fisher's budget or trust on a consultant, Jobin and Cary studied networking technology and spent weekends running wires through the company's offices. When the network was finally up and running, Jobin focused on the sales-lead problem. He brought in ACT!, a contact-management program from Symantec Corp. He oversaw the entry of every sales lead, along with information about each lead, into the database. Then he set up an 800 number that connected laptops on the road to information from the Dun and Bradstreet MarketPlace database on CD-ROM, which allowed salespeople in the field to get updated lead lists. The upshot: The average number of exposures before a sale closes has been cut from five to two. Emboldened by his success, Jobin talked Fisher into bringing on more new salespeople, many of them to work on international sales.

And then there was the World Wide Web. If you've ever tried explaining the Internet to your grandparents, you might be able to relate to what Jobin and Cary went through trying to convince the senior Fisher to back a company Web site. Cary gave up, but Jobin once again found a way to penetrate the obstinacy. He did a search on the Web and showed Fisher that other companies, including the Sharper Image, were already making money selling SpacePens on the Net. Particularly galling to Fisher was the discovery that someone who had worked for him was running a Web page that offered SpacePen seconds at a discount. Fisher called his lawyers—pausing only long enough to tell Jobin to get going on a Web site. The site (www.fisherpen.com/spacepen) went up in February 1996.

Jobin's efforts have paid off. In 1995, sales shot up from $3.5 million to $5.8 million. The administrative costs of sales—including Jobin's travel, phone calls, and Federal Express—have dropped 30 percent, not counting the thousands of dollars the company has saved on marketing materials since Jobin moved production of those materials in-house.

Not that success seems to have softened Fisher. Asked what he thinks about the role technology has played in his company's turnaround, Fisher looks up from admiring his pen collection and says, "I don't know what the hell you're talking about." But Jobin knows that whether he admits it or not, Fisher is catching on. The proof: He recently had a PC installed in a corner of his living room, not far from the astronaut memorabilia.

Financial Controls

The third important aspect of Internal Infrastructure is financial controls, the systems that are in place to monitor financial performance. At a minimum, every company should have accurate and current information on cash flow, accounts receivable and payable, operating margins, and forecasted financing needs for two to three years in the future.

This is another area that many entrepreneurs find to be of little interest. Most do not have any formal training in business or finance and must rely on others to supply the information. But it is crucial for every growing company to have an accounting system with cost-accounting capabilities to monitor and control cost and profit centers. This is especially critical in situations where price cuts or new lines of business are being considered. The various costs associated with each business unit must be identified, including labor, operating, and administrative costs, as well as allocation of indirect costs such as overhead.

For Diamond Courier Services, the business had diversified into six different business units, each with its own unique pricing and billing practices. The problem was that the CEO, Claudia Post, didn't know which if any of them were profitable. She was operating on a set of reasonable but *unexamined assumptions*. She assumed, for instance, that if she kept selling and priced her service at market rates, she would build a profitable business. Post assumed that growing volume would generate economies of scale. She assumed that if she took good care of customers, the business would take care of itself. She relied on those assumptions because, as she admits now, she had never taken the time to question or even test them. As a result Post continued to believe that sales were the company's salvation, when in fact nearly every sale she made pushed the company a little further into the red and a little closer to failure.

It is common to hear stories of businesses that cut prices, increased sales, and then went bankrupt. Fortunately for Diamond Courier, Post connected with a financial adviser who helped her build the cost-accounting tools her business needed, and then assisted her in making the tough decisions. In the two years since, the unprofitable revenue has been replaced by profitable business, revenue per job has more than doubled, and the business is in the black, with revenues of $3.5 million in 1997. But not every business gets the help it needs on time. For many, by the time they realize they need to pay more serious attention to the numbers, it's too late.

Now Post counts her blessings as well as her cash every night. "I could have just spun out," she says. She knows better now. "Look, I'm never going to be a serious financial person, but you own a business, it's your responsibility. I can't slough it off on somebody else. I have to know."

For companies with aggressive growth plans such as going public or expanding through mergers and acquisitions, finding a higher-level financial adviser to work with is vital. A chief financial officer can provide more sophisticated financial strategies (long-term financial plan, optimal financial structure, future value, etc.) required for these activities.

But the question is always "When?" When a company is growing quickly, it's often difficult to pinpoint the best time to bring on a new level of management. Waiting too long to hire a CFO can create problems, because growth strategies can be handicapped if a company fails to track its numbers adequately or impress prospective bankers and investors.

Unfortunately, there's no one-size-fits-all guideline that can tell entrepreneurs when it's time to improve their companies' in-house capabilities. "Whether or not you need a full-time CFO depends on a lot of different factors, including the financial expertise of the founder and his or her existing management team," observes Mark Sawicki, a vice-president at Virtual Growth Inc., an accounting firm based in New York City. "It also depends on how big your company is and how big you intend it to be and whether or not you expect to raise money from professional investors or the public markets."

Then there's that sticky issue of how much a growth company can afford to pay. "Some companies are so small, and will always be so small, that they're basically shoebox operations that will never need a CFO," says Sawicki. "Others need one early in order to achieve their growth goals, and if they're too small or too financially strapped to hire one through traditional means, they need to find one through a more flexible arrangement."

There are many "CFO for Hire" outfits springing up around the country, specifically because of this need for more sophisticated financial information among smaller growth companies. A part-time or out-sourced CFO can often be a good interim solution for companies whose staffing needs exceed their cash realities. Ask your CPA, business adviser, or local industry associations to recommend CFO-outsourcing organizations with good track records.

Clark Hubbard, the chief executive of $15 million CSI Data Systems, a value-added computer reseller in Norcross, Georgia, is a good example of a business owner who desperately needed a CFO's aid before his company could quite afford it. In 1995, Hubbard's company—then at about $4 million in sales—experienced a six-figure drop in inventory one month, causing Hubbard to suspect internal fraud. "I needed somebody to come in from the outside and examine all our financial operations in order to figure out what was happening and how to stop it quickly," he recalls.

Hubbard had the perfect candidate in mind: a friend who had worked for years as the CFO of a multinational corporation, only to lose his job after a merger. "He was extremely overqualified and way too expensive for us, but I trusted him completely. And he needed some work," Hubbard explains. "I told him, 'I sure as hell can't afford you, but if you'll accept the salary I can pay and give us top priority, I'll let you take on additional clients and meet with them at our offices.'"

The friend accepted the arrangement—and proceeded to revamp CSI's financial system, upgrade its accounting software, and solve the inventory shrinkage problem. "He set up a cash-management system for us so that extra funds get swept into an investment account each night," says Hubbard. "He also helped us establish a line of bank credit, which we'd never had before. Those two changes alone accomplished wonders on the cash-flow front and really helped us double our business in just a year."

Hubbard acknowledges he would have "probably never even thought about making the hire if the inventory crisis hadn't happened." However, when that first CFO left for a better-paying job, Hubbard promptly hired a replacement.

In an ideal world, business owners would hire CFOs before their companies reached some sort of financial crisis. Seth Godin, president and founder of Yoyodyne Entertainment in Irvington, New York, a creator of Internet promotions, did hire early. "Nearly two years ago it was clear that we wanted to switch from being a bootstrapped company to one with a broader capital base raised from professional investors," Godin says. "When those kinds of prospective investors ask to see your books, you can't exactly hand them a shoebox and a few postcards." As a short-term measure, Yoyodyne hired a part-time CFO to spend a half day each week at the company's offices. Then the company spent three months working with an executive-search firm to find the right CFO. "There are two kinds of accountants—one is ambitious and has career initiative, and I'm not really sure if that person should or shouldn't be a CFO," Godin says. "The other kind has the financial skills and also the flair and spark and marketing savvy to go out there and sell your company to the financial community. That's what we knew we needed."

Godin found his CFO. Yoyodyne also raised $4 million from a venture-capital group. The company intends to raise more money in the future, probably through an initial public offering of company stock. Godin's conclusion? "The right CFO is the perfect addition to your entrepreneurial team."

Options: The Right Staff

It's often difficult for business owners who lack specialized financial training to determine what type of expertise their companies require. Here's a quick checklist to help you analyze your company's needs:

Bookkeeper

A bookkeeper makes sense for a company that's quite young, quite small, or quite strapped for cash. Expect a bookkeeper to keep accurate if basic financial records—certainly detailed enough to help an outside accounting firm prepare taxes and, if needed, to do audited year-end financial statements. A bookkeeper should also be able to handle your accounts payable and receivable. Recruit a "full-charge" bookkeeper to get the highest level of expertise available at this level.

Controller

If significant growth is in your plans, you should hire a controller as quickly as you can afford to. That's because every growing company, even a young one, requires the skills a controller possesses, and it will grow faster with these skills available. A good controller can do everything a bookkeeper does but also much more—mainly because he or she is trained to have a larger perspective, beyond day-to-day numbers. Count on your controller to choose and maintain the right accounting software for your company, to generate timely weekly and monthly financial reports, and, of course, to keep cash flow on track with a well-run payables and receivables operation.

Chief Financial Officer

There's no hard and fast rule to tell you when to upgrade from a controller to a chief financial officer. "If all you need is a relatively small credit line from a local bank, hiring a CFO is probably unnecessary," explains Brian Benz, a chief financial officer with 13 years of experience at entrepreneurial companies. "But if you're going to be looking for a multilayered financing arrangement or dealing with professional investors or the public markets, or if you envision ongoing, complex financing deals like a long-term factoring relationship, then a well-qualified CFO will probably help." Expect your CFO to know how to navigate the various capital markets; the best candidates will have raised capital for at least one company before yours. A qualified CFO will be able to prepare a comprehensive business plan, complete with the kinds of financial and market projections investors look for. A competent CFO also knows how to handle in-person interviews with bankers and prospective investors. That will allow you to concentrate on what you do best: growing your company.

Source: Jill Andresky Fraser, "Hire Finance," *Inc.* January 1998, p. 87.

PUTTING IT ALL TOGETHER: ESTABLISHING METRICS TO MONITOR BUSINESS PERFORMANCE

What gets measured at your company? Is it primarily sales and profits? Or do you use other indicators to monitor the performance of the business in key areas? And how often do you track those measurements? There is an old saying, "what gets measured gets done." However, for many young growth companies, what gets measured is vague and uncertain.

As a company grows, it is constantly in a state of flux and change. Your business is a dynamic, creative enterprise with thousands of variables at play each day. Each of them has a pull on you and your employees, dictating their behavior and priorities. But at the end of the day, which are the really important variables? One of the most significant management tools for growing a company is the development of a clear set of performance indicators that are the criteria from which the business is managed and monitored. These critical numbers are most often associated with financial performance—sales, margins, accounts receivable. But other important aspects of your business also impact overall performance, such as customer service ratings, inventory, number of complaints, quality statistics, employee morale and satisfaction ratings, sales figures, and collections. Each company should reflect on what is most important to its business performance, and select a group of key indicators that are tracked on a regular basis.

A benefit of having a tracking system in place is that it forces management to become acutely aware of the most important aspects of the business; especially if not only do they have to report those numbers, but their compensation is tied to the performance. With management now thinking like owners, the business can be run independently of the owner's involvement on a day-to-day basis, which ensures that professional management is clear on performance expectations. It also minimizes "surprises" such as critical issues slipping through the cracks in the owner's absence.

Dan Caulfield of Hire Quality, a recruitment firm in Chicago that specializes in recruiting people who are leaving the military for civilian jobs, used to do all the thinking. He told everyone what information to get and how to get it, and even told the data-entry people how to key it in. He spent weeks training new staffers, telling them exactly what to do and how to do it. He drew up detailed instructions on everything from the steps to take to enlist job banks to the questions to ask job candidates. He held full-staff meetings every day at 8 A.M. and then again at 5 P.M. to find out exactly what was going on. He barely had time to think, yet he was unilaterally making all the decisions.

Then lightning struck. By 1996 the company had grown to $1 million in sales. Caulfield turned over the sales department to the lead salesperson, but after six months of his tenure, sales had begun to decline. Caulfield moved out of the corner office and into the sales office, planning to "lead by example." To him that meant continuing to tell the new manager what to do. "Make more cold calls," he advised.

The staff did. Sales plummeted, and the manager, one of his oldest and most valuable employees, handed in his letter of resignation.

"Suddenly it hit me." Caulfield says, "I wasn't leading by example; I was micromanaging people—just as I'd always done." In desperation he tried managing sales data instead of salespeople. He gathered every invoice he'd ever sent and began tracking things: the number of sales closed from cold calls, the number closed from clients calling them, descriptions of their best contracts and how they had gotten those contracts. The results from the analysis of that information couldn't have been clearer: "When prospects called us, we closed sales more than seventy-nine percent of the time. Obviously we needed to improve our marketing efforts to attract more quality prospects." So Caulfield laid out almost $400,000 on technology, installing a system centered on a massive database.

Hire Quality, which generated more than $5 million in revenues in 1998, now has 50 employees working in offices in Philadelphia, Washington, D.C., San Diego, and Los Angeles. Every week it registers 2,000 new job candidates and sends more than 600 preinterviewed candidates to work. Yet Caulfield manages the organization with just one 15-minute meeting a week and one 60-minute companywide address because everyone in the organization has access to the same information through the company's database. "I continue to marvel at how much more effective I am now that I spend my time concentrating on the right questions to ask, rather than on providing all the answers."

Performance indicators will be different for each company, depending on the type of business you are in and what is of particular importance to achieving success. Indicators should be chosen that represent the company's unique critical success factors (see Chapter 5, Clarity of Purpose) for sustaining competitive advantage in the marketplace, as well as tracking the general health of the business.

To help make the tracking reports user-friendly, make sure that the ones referred to most often are kept fairly short. For instance, you probably should only track four or five key indicators at the most on a daily basis—the ones that can have the most significant impact on the business. A more detailed report may be more appropriate for a monthly review. Areas to be considered for your company's performance measures may include:

- Customer feedback scores (service rating, or other important customer measures)
- Employee feedback scores (annual surveys measuring morale, commitment, etc.)
- Profit measures (look at key drivers of profitability to determine the most important operational/business functions that will impact profitability)
- Cash management (accounts receivable/payable, cash balances, inventory levels, future projections)
- Sales revenue growth (number of cold calls, close ratios, etc.)

Once the indicators have been selected, begin the measuring. You can track the numbers on a monthly, weekly, or even daily basis. Ron Friedman, CEO of Stonefield Josephson, an accounting firm in Santa Monica, California, argues that key numbers should be tracked daily. "Every morning by nine-thirty, I receive a printed report that tracks certain key results from the day before. That's a tremendous management advantage since I can respond immediately to any problem signals. Think of all the time and money you lose when you find out about problems only at the end of the week or the month." Friedman knows how those numbers should compare with daily target results. "Small fluctuations are only natural, but once you track daily results for a while, you'll get the feel for those fluctuations that are more troubling," he notes.

The development of a sound Internal Infrastructure is one of the most important keys to long-term growth. It allows information and communication to flow easily throughout your company, and it supports the company's strategy and the efforts of employees to perform at the highest level.

CHAPTER 8

Staying One Step Ahead

THE AIM OF THIS BOOK IS TO PROVIDE YOU WITH A practical framework and the management tools that will help you break through from your current level and reach the next level of growth. *Remember, you are in control of your company's future destination.* For better or worse, the quality of your decisions and actions as owner, entrepreneur, director, or manager will dictate your company's future success or failure. The diagnostic tools in the first two chapters of this book (At What Stage of Growth is Your Company? and The Growth Strategy Analysis) have helped you to assess your company's growth potential by identifying specific areas you need to work on. The tools and exercises provided in Chapters 3 to 7 can help you to build competence in each of the five Growth Drivers.

Using these tools and preparing your company to get to the next level won't be easy. It will take a lot of hard work, persistence, and determination to implement these management practices. And change won't happen overnight. But if you are diligent in applying the information laid out in this book, *you will create an extraordinary future for your business!*

There are three important things to remember as you begin to apply the results of the Growth Strategy Analysis (GSA) to your company. First: Don't try to do everything at once. You shouldn't tackle too many different initiatives at the same time—it will scare people, and may even backfire. Using your scores from the GSA and the information presented in the other chapters, *choose just two or three things to focus on changing or implementing*. Otherwise you will overwhelm yourself and your employees. The book provides plenty of self-assessment exercises to help you understand what the weakest points of your business or management are, and what is most likely to prevent your business from getting to the next level. Select two or three as priorities for the next three months, write them down, and work on them. Once you've made progress in those areas, then select another three projects, and focus on those. In this way you will slowly but surely build the business and prepare it for long-term growth. You will also build confidence and trust among your employees as they see commitment, follow-through, and lasting results in each of the areas you focus on.

Second, make sure that you involve your management team and employees in the process. Don't underestimate the insights, ideas, and knowledge that can come from your people. And believe me—they want to help you make the business more successful. Many of the exercises and examples provided in the book can and should involve the management team. Make them a part of the process of growth and change. Let them in on it. Solicit their input and involvement. You will be rewarded in the end.

Finally, if you need help, don't be afraid to ask for it. Many local and national-level business advisers stand ready to assist business owners make the critical transitions of growth. Some are experts in specific areas where you might need help, such as developing roles and responsibilities for employees, or installing information systems to monitor financial performance. Others are generalists—business management advisers who are good at seeing the big picture and helping you make critical business decisions. These individuals are better suited to advise you on issues such as Clarity of Purpose, Strategic Planning, and CEO coaching.

If you do decide to engage an adviser or consultant, take care during the selection process. Call some of the consultant's previous clients to assess track record and performance, and ask those references about specific outcomes and results of the consultant's work. Personal chemistry is important too, because hiring a consultant generally involves a high degree of communication and sharing otherwise private information about your business—so pay attention to your gut instincts as well as the references.

RESOURCES

By now you have identified your company's strengths and weaknesses and have a better understanding of its growth potential, and you are ready to put into practice some of the tools and exercises outlined in the previous chapters. This final chapter provides you with additional resources—books, Internet sites, organizations—that can help you delve deeper as you build your competency in each of the five critical growth areas. Many of these resources have been carefully screened and reviewed by the editorial staff at *Inc.*

The resources are grouped by Growth Driver: Market Intelligence, Strategic Leadership, Clarity of Purpose, Strategic Planning, and Infrastructure. There is also reference to *Inc.*'s own Internet resources on page 215.

Market Intelligence

Libraries, Books, and Directories

How does one explore libraries' mines of information? "Your single best first step is to find a good research librarian and buy him or her lunch. It's the librarians' job to help find answers, and they love to do it," says Jacqui Jenkins, director of the Small Business Development Center at the University of Pennsylvania's Wharton School of Business, in Philadelphia. Debra Malewicki, director of the University of Wisconsin's Innovation Center adds, "If you can define your problem even nebulously, the librarian can target your search. Most entrepreneurs haven't been in the library for a while. The technology has changed. There's information stored on CD-ROM now, and you can do database searches."

Visit a large public or university library first. Staffers there can introduce you to *RMA's Annual Statement Studies*, which gives income statements and financial ratios for four sizes of businesses in every major industry; *The Almanac of Business and Financial Ratios*, also published annually, which lists total receipts and 22 ratios for industries; *U.S. Census Data*, from both the popular census and the census of the retail trade, conducted every five years; *State and County Business Patterns*, which lists local businesses' sales, annual payroll, number of employees, and more; *Thomas Register*, which lists American manufacturers and their trademarks; the Standard Rate and Data Service's guide to direct-mail lists; Grey House Publishing's directory of catalog marketers; and online databases that show you what the media have said about your market and competitors. Also, the U.S. Patent and Trademark Office has designated libraries around the country to conduct patent searches.

Some libraries now offer *rent-a-researcher* programs, a reasonably priced option for those who've gotten as far as they can on their own. Information professionals at the Cleveland Public Library's fee-based service agency, the Cleveland Research Center (216-623-2999), consult not just public-library resources but government offices, university libraries, and 2,000 online databases. The center charges $60 an hour, with a 15-minute minimum, plus various pass-through costs.

If you're bothering the librarian too often, check the shelves for the *Small Business Sourcebook*, edited by Carol A. Schwartz (Gale Research, Detroit), an insider's guide through the tangle of resources. Profiles of 224 types of businesses target resources for everything from accounting services to yogurt shops. That last listing, for instance, points you to four sources of start-up information; four key associations; eight other associations, including the American Cultured Dairy Products Institute; such reference works as *The Very Best: Ice Cream and Where to Find It;* and information on suppliers.

After you emerge bleary-eyed from the library, reams of statistics under your arm, consider investing in these two books: *The Insider's Guide to Demographic Know-how* by Diane Crispell (Probus, 1990, $49.95), can help you understand what all those numbers say about your customers. *Do-It-Yourself Market Research*, by George E. Breen and Albert B. Blankenship (McGraw-Hill, 1989, $16.95), will help you collect your own numbers to augment big-picture data. It introduces readers to the fundamentals of market research, gives step-by-step instructions for conducting a research study, and includes many sample questionnaires.

Trade Associations

Trade associations may prove your best source of information, or they may prove useless; the only way to judge is to contact them. Even a mediocre association should point you toward some industry statistics, publications, and trade shows. Find trade associations listed in the *Gale's Encyclopedia of Associations* in the library, indexed by name and subject, or in the *Small Business Sourcebook.*

A trade group may also help identify your competitors. Although your competitors may one day be your enemies, for now consider them your well-informed friends—and hope they reciprocate. Chip Perfect has started three businesses in Lawrenceburg, Indiana: a ski resort, a warehousing facility, and a business incubator. In each case he found others in the industry more than willing to share thoughts about equipment and operating ratios. Those outside his market opened up more quickly, but when Perfect started his warehousing business, he spoke to the biggest local player in the industry. The competitor didn't mind a small company catching the little fish it threw back. "Its attitude was, we'll help you out as long as you recognize your place," says Perfect.

College and University Resources

Perfect also got help from university professors. "They've spent a lifetime studying your subject and are certainly eager to tell someone about it." When Perfect was planning his warehousing business, one professor listed five books on the subject and told him which one to read if he read only one (which he did). The professor also gave Perfect the names of industry contacts outside the area and a consultant who, in a free interview, provided Perfect with basic industry information. Professors in entrepreneurial studies can help with a range of issues (for a list of them, call the Program Office at the Small Business Administration, 202-205-6665).

Can't afford to hire the talent you need? Ask about student-consultants-for-hire programs at nearby business schools. For example, MBA candidates with Weatherhead Student Consultants, at Case Western's Weatherhead School of Management, in Cleveland, do project work for about $25 an hour for small companies and start-ups. And Stanford Business School's "New Ventures" course requires students to work on a project for a small or midsize company. Check other business schools; they're likely to have similar programs.

In addition, small-business institutes (SBIs) at colleges around the country can provide students who'll do some of your market-research legwork. Call the SBA for the name of an SBI near you.

Electronic Intelligence

There are sites on the Internet that businesspeople can use for do-it-yourself marketing research, to glean online details about competitors, industry trends, and customer opinions from the comfort of your keyboard. As a first step, type in a competitor's name, using an Internet search engine such as Yahoo!, AltaVista, HotBot, or Infoseek, and see what turns up. But what next? *Inc.* asked information brokers and others knowledgeable about the online world to recommend the best sites and services for conducting further competitive-intelligence research on the Internet. *Inc.* boiled their lists down to the following sites, which are relatively easy to use—and are free, unless otherwise stated.

Digital dossiers. The financial data on public companies that have always been available are even more accessible on the World Wide Web. Hoover's Online (www.hoovers.com) gives income statement and balance sheet numbers in detailed profiles of nearly 2,500 public companies. The service is free to America Online subscribers (keyword: Hoover), but otherwise costs $9.95 a month. However, Hoover's Online lets anyone download free half-page profiles of 10,000 (mostly public) companies.

For official filings from public companies, go to the U.S. Securities and Exchange Commission home page (www.sec.gov/) and tap into the SEC's Edgar database. When you need numbers fast, Edgar's a pal, but this system is not so easy on the eyes. Likewise, it's handy to have statistics on the *Fortune* 500 online (select *Fortune* from the menu at www.pathfinder.com/), but the site could be more user-friendly.

Avenue Technologies (www.avetech.com/avenue) packages news and numbers from 11,000 private and 9,000 public companies as well as 5,000 international companies. The reports, which draw on such sources as Moody's Investors' Service, cost $15 to $40 each, and the level of detail varies greatly. However, the Web site presents summaries, so you know what to expect before you buy. The first online report is free. Dun & Bradstreet's Online Access (www.dbisna.com/dbis/product/secure.html) provides short reports on 10 million U.S. companies, many of them privately held—but no credit ratings. (D&B subscribers can get full credit reports online for around $30.)

Real-time research. Getting news about small private competitors can be daunting, but it's not impossible. Ecola's 24-Hour Newsstand (www.ecola.com/news) links you to the Web sites of more than 2,000 newspapers, business journals, magazines, and computer publications. Click on Newspapers, for example, and you'll get a city directory; type in a rival company's home city, and a list of local papers appears. Of course, some of the periodicals are more easily searched than others, and some charge fees.

To track down obscure news, it may be worth perusing the pricey archives of hard-core online research services such as Dialog and Nexis. But for recent news, first try CNN Interactive (www.cnn.com). Information broker Stephanie Ardito recalls a client desperate to locate certain recent information on diabetes research. In vain, Ardito searched Dialog's pharmaceutical databases as well as several online news wires. Finally, she located the information at the CNN site. "They're right up to the moment," she says. One caveat: the CNN archives go back weeks but not years.

Some information brokers think The Knowledge Index, available to CompuServe members, represents a real deal at $21 an hour; others hate it, calling it a watered-down version of the almighty Dialog research service.

The Electric Library (www.elibrary.com) is also great for scouring magazines, reference works, and news wires, notes Mary Ellen Bates, the author of *The Online Desk Book*. Costing $9.95 a month, the service is designed for students; still, business users can take advantage of a two-week free trial worth 100 searches. Homework Helper, a similar service produced by the same company, is available on the Prodigy online service. Despite its name, Homework Helper is used by businesspeople and costs just $6 an hour or $9.95 a month for two hours, plus $2.95 for each additional hour.

MediaFinder (www.mediafinder.com) provides an index and description of thousands of newsletters, catalogs, and magazines. It contains a limited number of Web links.

The online grapevine. The ability to "listen in" on conversations about yourself or your competitors may represent one of the best market-research values of the Internet, simply because it's unique to the medium. These newsgroups and discussion groups are prevalent in the Usenet section of the Internet. The groups offer more than gossip; you can identify experts among the contributors.

Deja News Research Service (www.dejanews.com) claims to have the "largest collection of indexed archived Usenet news anywhere." Liszt (www.liszt.com) is a searchable directory of e-mail discussion groups. Both contain tips for Internet novices.

Business clearinghouses. Several Web sites contain good compilations of business resources and links to other Web sites. John Makulowich's

Awesome Lists (www.clark.net/pub/journalism/awesome.html) has links to more than 140 sites. American Demographics (www.demographics .com) maintains a directory of marketing experts. ProfNet (www.vyne .com/profnet) helps you quickly locate professors who are leaders in their fields.

StartingPoint (www.stpt.com/busine.html) features an extensive list of commercial directories and resources. Babson College (www. babson.edu) is in tune with small business people's needs. Finally, the Competitive Intelligence Guide (www.fuld) is worth looking at.

When the Internet isn't enough, consider the following subscription databases, recommended by information brokers for their ease of use:

- UnCover indexes nearly 17,000 publications; for $25 a year, the Reveal Alert service will e-mail you the tables of contents of your favorite journals. For more information, call 800-787- 7979, or go to www.uncweb.carl.org on the Web.

- ProQuest Direct lets users retrieve text and graphics from 25,000 publications. Call 800-521-0600, ext. 2705, or go to www.umi.com on the Web.

- DataTimes EyeQ includes a Private-Eye service for EyeQ sub- scribers that will track your competitors and report back for about $15 a month. Go to www.datatimes.com on the Web.

Finally, when you really need the information fast, hire a fact find- er. The information broker Ruth Orenstein of BiblioData, in Needham Heights, Massachusetts, publishes a helpful newsletter, *The Cyber- Skeptic's Guide to Internet Research.* Call 781-444-1154 for details. For a sample issue of the newsletter online, go to www.bibliodata.com.

Push Sites

Being pushy may be frowned upon in some circles, but in the Internet world, it's the hottest new concept. So-called push technology may be the best new hope for saving time. Instead of your going onto the Web in search of information, it comes to you—automatically. A big hit at the moment, push technology gathers news stories and other material based on criteria you set and then forwards them to you. It's like a personal clipping service, albeit one that's a little less able to dis- tinguish good from bad than an old-fashioned human being. But the point is that you don't have to do anything but read the material when it comes in. Push comes in two basic varieties: e-mail message and screen saver. Examples include My Yahoo (edit.my.yahoo.com/config/login), which sends you a daily news page customized to your interests, and PointCast, which, among other things, flashes news and stock quotes across your screen.

Another company, Individual Inc., offers a subscription to a customized electronic news service. For $29.95 a month per user, Individual's "Heads Up" service each day transmits to every subscriber the first few lines of articles that are relevant to their particular areas of interest. It will also transmit whole articles for an additional charge.

Although it has yet to reach its potential, push technology does offer you a steady stream of stories about companies or industries you want to track. Consider signing up for some of the free introductory offers of several services and then testing them.

Strategic Leadership

Peer Groups

You'll find groups in the local chapters of several national organizations that cater to the needs of top company officials. The hitches? You must meet strict membership terms and be willing to, as one CEO put it, "roll up your sleeves and get dirty." Here's a sampling:

The Young Entrepreneurs' Organization (YPO) (800-804-3688) has 40 chapters and requires members' companies to have sales of at least $1 million; new members must be under 39 years old. Annual costs vary according to chapter, but average $1,500. This educational, international networking group offers mentoring, peer groups, and monthly forums to its 600-plus members. Forums bring together 10 or so members and a moderator. The group, after pledging confidentiality, acts as an advisory board for members.

Young Presidents' Organization (800-773-7976) is for CEOs not older than 50 with at least 50 full-time employees and, generally, $7 million in sales. YPO charges $2,000 in annual dues, plus various local chapter fees. YPO supports more than 7,000 presidents, CEOs, and chairpersons of companies with approximately $5 million in sales and 50 full-time employees. Though its motto, "Better presidents through education and idea exchange," emphasizes its commitment to education and networking, the group, according to some, is more akin to a country club! To its credit, it extends programs to members' spouses. Many

YPO members, once they hit 50, graduate to the World Presidents' Organization, which emphasizes public service.

Inc. Eagles CEO Program (www.eaglesceo.com/content.html, 800-900-4441), a joint-venture of *Inc.* and Eagles, provides methods for CEOs of high-performance companies to collectively interact on strategic issues and generate solutions to help their businesses excel. Membership dues range from $2,700 to $3,600 per quarter, depending on company size. Eagles targets companies with over $10 million in annual sales. Members meet monthly to share intelligence, experiences, pinpoint their key concerns, and work jointly toward insightful solutions. The Eagles' mission is to make this the most valuable business day of the month for the CEO members. *Inc.* Eagles looks for CEOs who are ready to be challenged and held accountable to take their company to the next level; interested CEOs must apply via phone interview, and not all are accepted. As of September 1998, the program had groups in Boston, Tampa, Orlando, Dallas, Washington, D.C., Phoenix, and Chicago, and it was expanding nationally at a rapid pace.

TEC/the Executive Committee (www.tecceo.com; 800-274-2367) organizes peer groups nationwide for CEOs and presidents. Membership costs range from $5,400 annually (plus a $400 one-time enrollment fee), for companies with $750,000 to $3 million, to $8,700 annually (plus an $800 one-time fee) for those with more than $3 million in sales.

TEC chapters offer one-on-one coaching, seminars with speakers and consultants, and daylong executive sessions at which members have an opportunity to get solutions to their most gut-wrenching management problems from 14 peers, with the help of a facilitator. Steve Ashton, CEO of the photo-image printing company Ashton Photo, in Salem, Oregon, and a former TEC member, remembers the meeting at which he shared his financials. "Deciding which growth path the company should take was difficult. Luckily, I wound up with a consensus. You can't beat the feedback; it's wonderfully candid."

The Chief Executive Officers' Club at the Center for Entrepreneurial Management, founded and headed by Joseph Mancuso, (www.ceoclubs.org; 212-633-0060;) annually) is open to CEOs of all ages as long as they're nominated by a current member and run companies with at least $2 million in revenues. Its 450 members, in 12 cities, hear influential speakers and exchange company and personal information behind closed doors. Annual dues begin at $1,000.

The Council of Growing Companies (800-929-3165; www. ceolink.org) has 20 peer groups. The organization seeks high-growth companies with at least $3 million in sales.

The Women Presidents' Organization (212-818-9424; www. womeninc.com), run by Women Inc., operates 14 peer groups nationwide and charges $1,000 a year. Service businesses must have $1 million in sales; product-driven companies must have $2 million.

If those organizations don't appeal to you, hunt down local support networks. Many are listed in the Yellow Pages; you'll hear about others from fellow members of your trade associations. Of course, you needn't limit yourself to *your* industry's associations: your business problems will, we can assure you, be shared by members of the thousands of groups you'll find listed in library copies of *National Trade and Professional Associations of the United States* or *State and Regional Associations of the United States* (both from Columbia Books, in Washington, D.C.) and *Encyclopedia of Associations* (Gale Research).

Don't ease up in your search for the perfect networking group. Ashton Photo's CEO Steve Ashton met many like-minded, noncompeting company execs through his local Chamber of Commerce. His active role at the Chamber led him to his local economic development board, where he's now exposed to a larger pool of potential peers. Alternatively, you could visit CEOs at their own companies, phone friends and business associates, or tap the Lions and Rotary clubs and the Jaycees.

Unfortunately, not all CEO discussion groups are created equal. Two years ago, Craig Moreland joined a CEO peer group in hopes of finding insight and expertise that could help him grow his company. "Most of the people in my group were focused on daily firefighting rather than being strategic," laments Moreland, whose $2 million Newport Beach, California, company, Coast Label, manufactures custom labels and tags. "We were covering a lot of remedial things, like financial statements." Moreland spent a year in that group before switching to another, more sophisticated one. He had learned an important lesson: The wrong peer group can be a waste of time.

Keep in mind that the most successful peer groups generally have the following characteristics:

■ *Attract varied expertise.* Look for groups that offer a broad cross-section of skills and strengths. Nancy Hanson, president of Roxbury Mills, a 48-employee knitting mill in Far Rockaway, New York, belongs to a Women Presidents' Organization peer group that includes not only other manufacturers but also an architect, a designer, and the head of an advertising agency. "It's like an advisory group that helps me gain a different perspective," says Hanson. She is currently devising a new marketing strategy to sell a custom product through an 800 number—a plan that requires the kind of expertise she probably wouldn't find in a room full of manufacturers.

In industries in which most companies do business only locally, peer-group diversity can be geographical. Peter Schrader belonged to such a group of construction companies for eight years and declares that Schrader & Co., his $1.2 million remodeling company, "is far stronger and my skills are far more advanced than they would ever be without that network." Through his group, Schrader, in Burnt Hills, New York, found a mentor in California who showed him how to integrate design capability into his company.

■ *Stay small.* Experts agree that 10 to 15 people is an ideal size for a CEO peer group. With more members than that, you may spend most of your time waiting to be heard. Find out exactly how many members are permitted in a group, and beware of organizations that justify larger numbers because "not everyone comes all the time." A peer group with a spotty attendance record won't develop an atmosphere of trust and won't provide you with a consistent sounding board.

■ *Stress confidentiality.* "At every meeting, we ask if anyone knows of any breaches of confidentiality," says Keith Alper, president of Creative Producers Group and a member of a Young Entrepreneurs' Organization (YEO) peer group. Loose lips get you kicked out of his group. "It's a totally open forum to discuss anything," says Alper, whose corporate-communications company is based in St. Louis. "It's almost like a religious experience, and confidentiality is absolutely sacred." Sound extreme? Maybe so, but it's a way to remind members to be discreet. Some groups will even ask you to sign a confidentiality agreement.

■ *Clearly define "peers."* You may think of your peers as CEOs who run companies as big as yours or who are in related industries. But not all peer groups have the same definition. Mark Helow, president of the *Inc.* Eagles CEO Program, based in Boston, generally groups companies by annual sales volume. Other organizations might put small and large companies together.

■ *Expect accountability on the part of members.* "If the group gives you suggestions, you must come back to the next meeting and report on what you've done," says Jim Schell, who runs Opportunity Knocks, a peer-group organization based in Bend, Oregon. An effective peer group puts you on the spot by demanding to know what you've done lately. "One of our group members knew he had to make a termination," recalls Ray Silverstein. "At the next meeting, the first thing his peers asked was, 'Well, did you do it?' The group forces you to take action you don't always want to take."

■ *Don't stress business generation.* While it's natural for business relationships to evolve within CEO peer groups, that should never be your primary motivation for joining—because your desire to present your company in a positive light might prevent you from discussing your problems and weaknesses openly. "We have an agreement that no one in the group is allowed to solicit business from any other member," says Steven Krauser, who runs Network Associates, a CEO peer organization based in Hicksville, New York. "I was in there for thirteen months before anyone would even refer me," says Joseph Cosgrove, the director of Coronado Travel, in Roslyn, New York, and a Network Associates member. The son-in-law at a $20 million family-owned travel agency, Cosgrove has discussed succession issues with his group.

■ *Stick to a consistent format.* Most peer groups meet monthly for anywhere from a few hours to a full day. A typical agenda might include follow-up from the last meeting, a guest speaker, a visit to a member's company, or a detailed discussion of one company's most pressing issue. Pricier groups, such as TEC, also entitle you to a few hours of between-meeting consulting time with your facilitator or another expert. What format will suit you? How long can you afford to be away from the office? Do you want members of your group visiting your company? If there are guest speakers, will they address topics that interest you? Is the format flexible enough to deal with unforeseen crises?

■ *Have good facilitators.* A facilitator's job is to prevent entrepreneurs from monopolizing the conversation, leaning toward self-obsession, or dodging the tough questions. "Seventy-five percent of the success or failure of one of our meetings is due to the facilitator," says Jim Schell of Opportunity Knocks. "You have to be able to extract the valid points from the meeting, bring out the quiet people, and shut up the noisy ones."

What if you form your own group? Even then you'll probably need some type of moderator. The Phoenix Network, a nationwide group of 24 public-relations companies, annually elects a president who helps set agendas and facilitates its biannual meetings to "make sure we stay on task with the issues we've agreed to cover," says president David Neuger. PrezNet, a peer group formed by company owners in Lincoln, Nebraska, also opted to hire an outside facilitator.

■ *Encourage trying before buying.* Ask to sit in on a peer-group meeting before you join. To protect confidentiality, the group probably won't allow you to remain for the entire meeting, but you should be able to stay long enough to gauge the chemistry in the room. If, after you've joined, you feel strongly that you've misjudged your choice, don't be afraid to make a change. Many peer groups stay together for years, but even their biggest boosters concede that it's important to assess regularly the return on your investment of time, energy, and money. Peter Schrader, for instance, values his Business Networks group but feels it is time to take a break. "I now have a very clear vision of what I want to accomplish," he says, "and I desperately need the time to implement it."

Considering joining a CEO discussion group? Watch out for these warning signs:

Red Flags—Peer-Group Pitfalls

■ *High turnover among group members.* Peer groups should place a premium on relationship building—and that's impossible when people are coming and going every month. Look for a group that accepts new members every six months or, better yet, once a year.

■ *Advice that isn't based on actual experience.* Entrepreneurs are notorious for being opinionated, but opinions aren't necessarily a result of knowledge. "We have a rule in our YEO group that you're not supposed to give advice. You're just supposed to relate your own experience," says Keith Alper of Creative Producers Group, in St. Louis. "If people give advice and they're not knowledgeable, that can be very damaging."

■ *Instant intimacy.* Peer groups foster an atmosphere of immediate camaraderie that's easy to abuse. Be wary of peers who try to solicit your business or ask for business referrals before you've had the chance to build up trust.

- *Your own impatience.* Can't wait to get your concern on the table? Not so fast. "It's very helpful to be a listener," notes Business Networks member Peter Schrader. "Everything that's said, you take back with you. Sometimes it makes you think, 'This is something I ought to clean up at my company, too.'"

Business Conferences/Educational Programs for CEOs

The Harvard Owner/President Management (HOPM) Program (800-HBS-5577, ext. 6009, inside the United States; or 617-495-6555, ext. 6009, outside the country) is run by the Harvard Business School. HOPM is a comprehensive management program open to owners and executives with at least 10 years of management experience whose companies have revenues of three million to several hundred million dollars. About 2,400 businesspeople have so far completed the nine-week program, which is held in three-week segments over a three-year period.

Another multiyear educational conference for CEOs is offered by the combined efforts of Massachusetts Institute of Technology, the Young Entrepreneurs Organization, and *Inc.* magazine. The three-year program, called "Birthing of Giants," is limited to CEOs of growing companies who are under 40 years of age. Registration is handled by *Inc.* Conferences (800-255-1080).

Inc. Conferences (www.inc.com/conferences; 800-255-1080) offers eight national conferences each year for managers of growing companies on topics such as financing growth, marketing strategies, managing people, and customer service strategies. The cost for the two-day conferences starts at $995, with additional fees for optional full-day workshops offered before and after the main conference.

Of particular interest to CEOs is *Inc.*'s CEO Symposium, a four-day meeting that combines speakers, workshops, and peer-group discussions. The conference is geared exclusively to CEOs and owners of growth companies, and is offered two times each year.

Business Coaching

Many CEOs, rather than using peer groups, prefer a one-on-one advisory relationship with a mentor or an objective business adviser. Such relationships are referred to as coaching. Finding the right coach may be difficult, but the industry's two largest professional groups do offer help. The International Coaching Federation (ICF) offers an online referral service at its Web site (www.coachfederation.org), as well as a free biweekly newsletter, *Coaching News*. Annual dues for membership in the ICF are $50.

Cheryl Richardson, a coach based in Newburyport, Massachusetts, recommends that anyone hiring a coach follow these guidelines: (1) Interview at least three coaches and check their credentials. (How long have they been coaching? What training have they received?) (2) Make sure a coach either has achieved the goal you're after or has coached others who have. (3) Get references and talk to them. Dan Kennedy, a Seattle-based coach, contends that the best coaches actually have coaches themselves. "They realize there's always more to learn about coaching," he says.

Coaching at its best employs a combination of talents too delicate for most books, which typically bring a towel-snapping sensibility to the topic. One exception: *Coaching for Performance,* by John Whitmore (Nicholas Brealey Publishing; distributed by the LPC Group, 800-533-0301; $15.95), originally published in 1992, and came out in a second edition in 1997. Whitmore captures and dissects the skill that sets the most effective coaches apart: using effective questioning to bring on increased awareness.

Board of Directors

Looking for a valuable legal resource on forming a board of directors? Consider the American Bar Association's *The Corporate Director's Guidebook* (312-988-5522, 1994, $19.95). It has an overview of directors' responsibilities, explains how to set up a board, and spells out the legal consequences.

Also try the National Association of Corporate Directors (NACD) (202-775-0509), which is a nonprofit organization focused on serving individuals working on company boards. An annual membership fee of $425 per person includes access to many educational programs (with titles such as, "The Effective Board in the Entrepreneurial Company"), plus various NACD publications, including a monthly newsletter.

Clarity of Purpose

The best place to find thought-provoking information on developing a clear purpose and direction for your business is from the guru on the subject, Jim Collins. In addition to an article in *Inc.* magazine ("What Comes Next?," October 1997), Collins, with partner Jerry Porras, has authored the best-selling book *Built to Last,* as well as the

Harvard Business Review article "Building Your Company's Vision" (September–October 1996). All three of these are well worth the read for those who would like to explore their company's core purpose and direction in greater depth.

Strategic Planning

Books

There are many books that offer assistance with planning. The classic that many experts prefer is *Strategic Planning: What Every Manager Must Know* (Free Press, 800-223-2348; $16), by George A. Steiner. Also useful for strategic planning novices is *Business Plans to Game Plans: A Practical System for Turning Strategies into Action,* by Jan B. King (Merritt Publishing, 800-638-7597; $29.95). *The Executive Guide to Strategic Planning,* by Patrick J. Below (Jossey-Bass, 800-956-7739) is also a favorite. Another book that aims to keep you firmly planted in your own particular corporate realities *is Total Business Planning,* by E. James Burton and W. Blan McBride (John Wiley). This 245-page paperback is full of question-and-answer quizzes that could prove useful in helping you think about growing your business; some examples are: What Business Are We In? Where Are We? Where Are We Going? How Do We Get There? and How Do We Know When We Are There? At $19.95, it's a more economical way to start than hiring a consultant.

For solid guides to basic business planning, consider three best-sellers published by *Inc.* magazine (*Inc.* Business Resources, 800-468-0800, ext. 5569; each $19.95): *The Guide to Retail Business Planning,* developed in conjunction with the Association of Small Business Development Centers (ASBDC); *The Service Business Planning Guide,* also an ASBDC/*Inc.* collaboration; *How to Really Create a Successful Business Plan* (3rd edition), which includes analyses and critiques of real-life plans.

Seminars

Some may profit greatly by attending a seminar on planning, which introduces you to a template that you can use at your own company. The American Management Association (AMA) offers 13 two- and three-day seminars that cover various elements of Strategic Planning (up to $1,495 for members and $1,720 for nonmembers). Contact the AMA at P.O.

Box 319, Saranac Lake, NY 12983-0319, Attn: Customer Service. Or call 800-262-9699. Information is also available on the AMA's Web site at www.amanet.org.

Peer Group

The Council of Smaller Enterprises (COSE), based in Cleveland, offers a strategic planning program through which 30 company owners team up with past graduates of the course, who serve as their mentors. The price is $2,995, and courses are held in Cleveland, Dayton, and Louisville. Call COSE at 216-621-3300, ext. 244.

Infrastructure

Organizational Structure

Finding others who have dealt with the personnel-related problems you confront may be the quickest way to get the help you need. The Society for Human Resource Management, in Alexandria, Virginia, sponsors MemberNet, a networking service that connects you with 3,500 society members who serve as volunteer consultants on various human-resources issues. "Rather than having to reinvent the wheel, you can pick up the phone and call someone and ask questions," says Adina Marcheschi, formerly of CPS Employment Services Network, in Westchester, Illinois. A single membership costs about $160 a year. Call 703-548-3440.

Employees: How to Find and Pay Them, an 18-page publication from the U.S. Small Business Administration, provides answers to some basic questions about interviewing candidates, using temp services, and establishing fair pay. The latest edition was published in spring 1998. (SBA Publications, P.O. Box 465621, Denver, CO 80201; 800-827-5722; www.sba.gov; $3).

On the topic of hiring, try *Hiring the Best*, by Martin John Yate (Bob Adams; 617-767-8100 $9.95). "There are a ton of books out there on the subject of hiring, but three-quarters of them are baloney," says Larry Murphy, in-house staffing consultant and hiring specialist at Cabletron Systems, in Rochester, New Hampshire. Murphy says that Yate's book addresses the needs, values, and desires of "the new work force," roughly defined as 25-to 35-year-olds who work in companies built around new technologies. But you don't have to be in high tech to appreciate the book. Murphy says it has helped him think in general about the sort of individual best suited to each job.

Another 1998 winner is Dr. Pierre Mornell's *Hiring Smart! How to Predict Winners and Losers in the Incredibly Expensive People-Reading Game* (Ten Speed Press, P.O. Box 7123, Berkeley, CA 94707; 800-841-2665; $24.95). Mornell is a psychiatrist who has developed some fail-safe methods for predicting behavior, which translate into practical approaches for screening, interviewing, and hiring the right people.

Job Descriptions

Job Description, a CD-ROM from Workscience Corp. (757-336-1109; www.workscience.com; $495), draws a highly detailed picture of nearly 33,000 job titles. Say you need an assistant controller. You might begin by pulling up the dictionary of occupational titles and selecting the numerical code for controller or by conducting a keyword search, typing in "controller," "comptroller," or "financial manager." The software responds by enumerating the title's traditional responsibilities, ranking skills on a scale from one to six, recommending training and education, and noting what sorts of temperaments do well in the job. When you're finished, you can import the search results into a word-processing document and distribute them to other staff members for comments.

Financial Controls

"What is ABC?," a free three-page executive brief on activity-based costing, is a useful tool for companies whose overhead is growing as fast as their direct costs, and is available from ABC Technologies, in Beaverton, Oregon (800-882-3141). A 16-page manufacturing case study can be obtained free from Small Business Forum (800-419-5018). To see how the practice works in service companies, order a reprint of "Tracking Costs in a Service Organization," published by Management Accounting (800-638-4427 ext. 280; $2.50) in 1993.

Accounting and Financial Fundamentals, by Robert Rachlin and Allen Sweeny (AMACOM, 800-262-9699; $19.95), covers the basics of cost accounting, the contribution concept, and other management tools. Service company owners and managers should check *Priced to Sell,* by Herman Holtz (Upstart, 800-829-7934; $27.95).

Online: A primer on how to do a business-unit "contribution margin analysis" is available on *Inc.* Online in the Interactive Worksheet area. The worksheet is titled, "Is a Product or Customer Costing More Than It's Worth?"

Cash and Operational Controls

Newcomers to cash flow should start with "Understanding Cash Flow," a 10-page pamphlet you can pick up from your local Small Business Administration office for about $1.

"Internal Controls for Protection and Profit," a reprint of an eight-page article from the *Small Business Forum* (Fall 1990), establishes the importance of controls for small-business owners. It focuses mainly on employee theft, using case studies. A list of resources at the end covers different aspects of controls. *Small Business Forum* reprints are $4 each; call 608-263-3166.

In *Coopers & Lybrand Guide to Growing Your Business,* the chapter on accounting systems and controls alone, explained in everyday English, might justify the $23 price tag. It is available from offices of C&L, which has devoted considerable resources to small business. Call 818-609-7117.

If you're easily intimidated by numbers, and terms like "average days outstanding" make you dizzy, *Cash Flow Problem Solver,* by Bryan Milling (Sourcebooks, 630-961-2161; $19.95) is the book for you.

Small Business Survival Guide (3rd edition), by Robert Fleury (Sourcebooks, 630-961-2161; $17.95) is good for its heavy emphasis on cash management.

For an introduction to pricing and cost analysis, start with "Improving Decision Making with Simple Break-even Analysis" (*Small Business Forum,* Spring 1990), a simple, easy-to-read article that serves as an introduction to the often-burdensome task of pricing and cost analysis (608-263-3166; $4).

Technology and Automation

If you're looking for some outside help with office automation, a worthwhile starting point is the Independent Computer Consultants Association (ICCA), a St. Louis–based trade group with 1,500 geographically diverse members, most of whom have at least 10 years of experience. Most members will do an initial consultation free of charge. Their Web site, www.icca.org, contains a complete membership list with links to each consultant's home page or e-mail address. ICCA's telephone number is 314-892-1675 or 800-774-4222.

Another major trade organization, the Information Technology Association of America (ITAA), also runs a Web site (www.itaa.org) listing members and featuring numerous articles about industry trends and issues. ITAA's phone number is 703-522-5055.

Employee handbooks

The following are useful titles:

How to Write Your Employee Handbook, by Stephen D. Bruce (Business & Legal Reports, 800-727-5257, ext. 169; $129.95).

Guide to Employee Handbooks, by Robert J. Nobile (Warren Gorham Lamont, 800-950-1216; $180).

The Employee Handbook Audit, by the Alexander Hamilton Institute (201-587-7050, $65.95; book and computer diskette for IBM or compatible are $96.95).

Compensation

Many good books are available to help you set up an incentive program. *The Game of Work,* 3rd edition, by Charles Coonradt (The Game of Work, 800-438-6074; $19.95), offers practical advice and is a pleasant read. Karen Jorgensen's *Pay for Results* (Merritt Publishing, 800-638-7597; $29.95) includes many helpful worksheets, forms, and checklists that will aid in the design process.

The Reward Plan Advantage, by Jerry McAdams (Jossey-Bass, 800-956-7739; $29.95), shows busy managers how to craft reward systems that promote initiative, productivity, and old-fashioned hard work. If you would like your employees to think and act like business owners, this book will help you design and implement incentives to get them to do so. McAdams, the national practice leader for reward and recognition systems at Watson Wyatt Worldwide, in St. Louis, urges readers to skip around in the book. Starting from scratch? The early chapters explain how to meld incentive plans with business-plan objectives. Planning to reevaluate an existing plan's raison d'être and return on investment? Use Chapter 4 as a diagnostic to see whether the plan still serves its intended purpose. There's no lack of tips on eliciting feedback from employees, because, as McAdams points out, the goal is to involve them in the process. The book also includes proven tips and tactics for design and implementation of employee incentive plans.

OTHER RESOURCES AVAILABLE FROM *INC.*

Inc. Online, The Web Site For Growing Companies (www.inc.com), has extensive resources for entrepreneurs, including 10 years of *Inc.* archives; special guides to finance, business technology, the Internet, and international business, a Local Business News area; bulletin boards; interactive worksheets; business databases; free software; and more.

Inc. Online offers full free access to original feature stories; an area for any business to build and store (for free) a Web site; nine active bulletin boards for peer-to-peer discussion; interactive worksheets; business databases and software; business Web links; a full-service *Inc.* 500 area with searchable databases of 16 years of winners and application information; an *Inc.* products store; and sign-up information for the large number of *Inc.*-sponsored national conferences, seminars, and expos.

THE NEXT LEVEL ONLINE:
www.inc.com/thenextlevel

THE NEXT LEVEL WAS DESIGNED TO BE INTERACTIVE—to give you a set of tools to help you assess your company's growth potential, and then to create a customized roadmap for managing growth successfully in the future. But it doesn't end there. *Inc.* has also set up a special Web site that is dedicated exclusively to those who read this book and are implementing new changes as a result.

The power of the *Inc.* brand is derived from more than just the quality of the magazine, conferences, books, or videos it produces. The real leverage comes from the *community* that *Inc.* has created among company builders, entrepreneurs, and managers of growing companies. A dynamic exchange takes place when entrepreneurs have the opportunity to share stories—to see how one manager overcame a challenge that another is now grappling with—and to support and sometimes challenge one another through the ups and downs of managing a growing company. Although *The Next Level* provides a framework for discussing business growth, the real practical teaching comes from the ongoing, cumulative real-life experiences of this community of entrepreneurs. This is where we hope the inspiration, motivation and learning from this book will be most salient.

I invite you to join your peers from all across the globe, and to meet electronically at **www.inc.com/thenextlevel**. There you can interact with and exchange ideas with those who, like you, are attempting to improve their companies' performance. You will have the opportunity to compare notes with other CEOs and managers through chat rooms and bulletin boards. You will also find interactive tools; case studies to read;

and additional material, resources, and links that will enhance the content of the book. And most importantly, the Web site will make the information in this book more practical, relevant and meaningful.

Let's continue this discussion online—at **www.inc.com/ thenextlevel.**

INDEX